The $13 Trillion Question

The $13 Trillion Question
How America Manages Its Debt

David Wessel

EDITOR

BROOKINGS INSTITUTION PRESS
Washington, D.C.

The Brookings Institution is a private nonprofit organization devoted
to research, education, and publication on important issues of domestic
and foreign policy. Its principal purpose is to bring the highest quality
independent research and analysis to bear on current and emerging
policy problems. Interpretations or conclusions in Brookings publica-
tions should be understood to be solely those of the authors.

Library of Congress Cataloging-in-Publication data

Names: Wessel, David, editor.
Title: The $13 trillion question : how America manages its debt /
    David Wessel, editor.
Other titles: Thirteen trillion dollar question
Description: Washington, D.C. : Brookings Institution Press, [2016] |
    Includes bibliographical references and index.
Identifiers: LCCN 2015034769 | ISBN 9780815727057 (pbk. : alk.
    paper) | ISBN 9780815727064 (epub) | ISBN 9780815727071 (pdf)
Subjects: LCSH: Debts, Public—United States. | Finance, Public—
    United States. | Fiscal policy—United States. | Monetary
    policy—United States.
Classification: LCC HJ8101 .A4155 2016 | DDC 336.3/40973—dc23
LC record available at http://lccn.loc.gov/2015034769

9 8 7 6 5 4 3 2 1

Typeset in Minion Pro

Composition by Westchester Publishing Services

CONTENTS

About the Hutchins Center on Fiscal and Monetary Policy

The Hutchins Center on Fiscal and Monetary Policy provides independent, nonpartisan analysis of fiscal and monetary policy issues in order to improve the quality and effectiveness of those policies and public understanding of them. It draws on the expertise of Brookings Institution scholars and of experts in government, academia, think tanks, and business, as well as the guidance of its Advisory Council. By commissioning research, convening private and public events, and harnessing the power of the Internet, it seeks to generate new thinking, promote constructive criticism, and provide a forum for reasoned debate. The Center was founded with a gift from the Hutchins Family Foundation.

ACKNOWLEDGMENTS

In addition to the fine authors and commenters included in the chapters that follow, we are grateful to the many others who contributed to this book. Several of the chapters were first presented as working papers at a Hutchins Center on Fiscal and Monetary Policy event at the Brookings Institution in September 2014. The conference versions of those papers were improved upon by contributions from copyeditor Martha Schultz and Hutchins Center staff Emily Parker and Parinitha Sastry. Special thanks to research assistant Brendan Mochoruk, who pulled together many parts from many contributors and helped turn the papers into a cohesive book. At the Brookings Institution Press, director Valentina Kalk, editorial director Bill Finan, and managing editor Janet Walker ushered the book through publication, with the help of John Donohue, project editor at Westchester Publishing Services.

PREFACE

Robin Greenwood, Samuel G. Hanson, and David Wessel

There is a lot of attention on the size and growth of the federal debt, and for good reason. The U.S. Treasury is the world's biggest borrower. As of fall 2015, it had run up a debt of more than $13 trillion, not counting the money the government owes to Social Security and other government trust funds. In the fiscal year that ended September 30, 2015, the federal debt increased by $725 billion, a sum larger than the economic output of all but the world's twenty largest economies.[1] Measured as a share of the nation's economic output, the federal debt today is larger than at any time since the end of World War II. Despite the growing concern about the fiscal health of the U.S. government, Treasury bills, notes, and bonds are still the world's most widely held and trusted debt securities.

There is much less attention paid to *how* the Treasury borrows all this money—how much is borrowed short-term and how much long-term, how much is borrowed at fixed interest rates and how much at rates that vary with inflation, and so on. These debt management decisions are the subject of intense scrutiny by bond traders, sophisticated institutional investors,

1. Table S-13, "Federal Government Financing and Debt," *Fiscal Year 2016 Budget of the U.S. Government* (www.whitehouse.gov/sites/default/files/omb/budget/fy 2016/assets/tables.pdf).

and a small cadre of technocrats at the U.S. Treasury and the Federal Reserve, but are largely ignored by Congress, the press, and the public. Yet the way that Treasury borrows affects us all. Debt management decisions can have a large impact on the long-run fiscal health of the U.S. government. They can influence the interest rates we pay when we borrow or the rates we earn when we save. And because the structure of government debt impacts how others in the financial system behave, debt management can affect the stability of the broader financial system.

Treasury debt management drew considerable attention in the early 1990s when Salomon Brothers was accused of manipulating the auctions that Treasury uses to borrow money, transgressions that led to a $290 million fine for Salomon, the resignation of its chief executive, the eventual sale of the company—and to more transparency in the way the Treasury borrows money. But the domains of U.S. monetary policy, fiscal and debt management policy, and the prudential regulation of financial intermediaries remained separate and distinct. The president and Congress chose the level of the budget deficit. The Treasury decided in what maturity and form federal debt would be issued. The Federal Reserve determined the level of short-term interest rates with a view toward steering the economy away from recession and high rates of inflation. And supervisory authorities regulated the capital and liquidity of banks and other financial intermediaries.

With the onset of the financial crisis in 2007 and 2008 and the subsequent easing of monetary policy, the clean lines between these domains have blurred. Once short-term interest rates hit the zero lower bound, conventional monetary policies lost their impact. As a result, the Federal Reserve resorted to quantitative easing (QE)—purchases of long-term Treasury bonds in the open market—to support aggregate demand. Because QE works by shortening the maturity structure of debt instruments that private investors have to hold, the Fed effectively entered the domain of debt management policy. And with the decision to pay interest on central bank reserves, the nearly $3 trillion of reserves on bank balance sheets have become the functional equivalent of Treasury bills not reflected in Treasury debt statistics. This blurring of functions suggests the need to reconsider the principles underlying government debt management policy.

Each of the three chapters in this book focuses on an important, and understudied, aspect of the principles underlying debt management. The chapters, and the comments that follow, are drawn from conferences held in 2014 by the Hutchins Center on Fiscal and Monetary Policy at Brookings and the U.S. Treasury—though they don't represent the positions of either institution.[2]

In chapter 1, Robin Greenwood, Sam Hanson, Josh Rudolph, and Larry Summers argue that optimal debt management policy balances a number of considerations. First, debt managers attempt to achieve a low cost of financing for taxpayers over time. For instance, the public benefits when debt is issued in forms that investors are eager to hold and, therefore, the debt carries a lower interest rate. As a number of authors have suggested, short-term Treasury bills have many of the same valuable properties as traditional money and therefore command a liquidity premium. As a result, short-term debt may be a "cheaper" form of financing than long-term debt. Second, it is desirable for the government to reduce the risks associated with government financing. Issuing longer-term debt may help insulate future taxes and spending from fluctuations in interest rates while also guarding against the possibility, albeit remote, of a self-fulfilling debt rollover crisis. Third, to the extent that changes in the maturity structure of the debt influence long-term interest rates and other asset prices, reductions in the average maturity of the debt are likely to have an expansionary impact on the economy—a consideration that looms large when monetary policy becomes constrained by the zero lower bound. Fourth, changes in the supply of short-term, money-like government debt may impact the amount of liquidity transformation pursued by private financial firms which, in turn, has potential ramifications for financial stability.

Their evaluation of these issues suggests that, on average, the case for the government issuing shorter-term debt is stronger and the case for maturity extension is weaker than generally supposed. They develop arguments that (1) by issuing shorter-term debt the government can generate substantial savings over time; (2) shortening the average maturity would only modestly increase fluctuations in the fiscal deficit, and the gains from reducing the volatility of these fluctuations are arguably small; and (3) an increased supply of short-term government debt is likely to enhance financial stability by counteracting the financial system's tendency toward excessive liquidity transformation.

Notwithstanding their general argument in favor of a shorter maturity of the government debt, Greenwood, Hanson, Rudolph, and Summers note that

2. "Debt Management in an Era of Quantitative Easing: What Should the Treasury and the Fed Do?," September 30, 2014 (www.brookings.edu/events/2014/09/30-debt-management-quantitative-easing-treasury-fed), and U.S. Treasury 2014 Roundtable on Treasury Markets and Debt Management, December 5, 2014.

the three forces listed above vary over time. In particular, current estimates of the cost savings from issuing shorter-term debt are quite low by historical standards.

In response to these arguments, Janice Eberly of Northwestern University's Kellogg School of Management, who served as assistant Treasury secretary for economic policy from 2011 to 2013, lauds the authors for identifying traditional and new objectives for Treasury debt managers, but underscores the difficulties in weighing and quantifying the trade-offs the debt managers must make. Brian Sack, who ran the markets desk at the Federal Reserve Bank of New York and now is at hedge fund D. E. Shaw, while sympathetic to much of the argument made in the chapter, objects to one of their four objectives for the Treasury debt managers (managing aggregate demand) and identifies several challenges involved with applying their framework in practice.

Chapter 2, also by Greenwood, Hanson, Rudolph, and Summers, points out that at the same time the Federal Reserve was shortening the maturity of debt in public hands through quantitative easing, the Treasury was extending the average maturity of the debt to mitigate fiscal risks associated with the government's growing debt burden. The Treasury's actions operated as a kind of reverse quantitative easing, replacing money-like short-term debt with longer-term debt.

Despite successive rounds of QE, the stock of government debt with a maturity over five years that is held by investors (excluding the Fed's holdings) has risen from 8 percent of GDP at the end of 2007 to 15 percent at the middle of 2014. Between two-thirds and three-quarters of the increased supply of longer-term Treasuries reflects the borrowing that the Treasury did to finance large budget deficits during and after the Great Recession. But the remaining one-quarter to one-third is due to the Treasury's explicit decision to extend the average maturity of it debt.

The authors also note, with disapproval, that current institutional arrangements mean that neither the Fed nor the Treasury views debt management policy on the basis of the overall national interest. In discussions of QE, the Federal Reserve has focused purely on the effects that its bond purchases were expected to have on long-term interest rates and, by extension, the economy more broadly. However, in doing so, it completely ignored any possible impact on government fiscal risk, even though the Federal Reserve's profits and losses are remitted to the Treasury. Conversely, Treasury's debt management announcements and the advice of the Treasury Borrowing Advisory

Committee (TBAC) have focused on the assumed benefits of extending the average debt maturity from a fiscal risk perspective and largely ignored the impact of policy changes on long-term yields. To the extent that the Federal Reserve and Treasury ever publicly mention the other institution's mandate, it is usually in the context of avoiding the perception that one institution might be helping the other achieve an objective. Specifically, the Fed does not want to be seen as monetizing deficits, while the Treasury has been reluctant to acknowledge the Fed as anything more than a large investor.

Before QE was launched in 2008, changes in Fed holdings of long-term bonds had only a tiny impact on the amount of long-term Treasury debt held by the public. However, the authors describe a few historical examples in which the Federal Reserve and the Treasury agreed to coordinate policy for the purpose of achieving a common set of objectives with regard to debt management. Thus, history suggests that greater cooperation on debt management is possible and prudent, the authors say.

The case that Greenwood, Hanson, Rudolph, and Summers make is provocative. To put it in perspective, four observers with relevant experience in the private and public sectors offer comments. Mary John Miller, who helped manage the federal debt at Treasury from 2010 to 2014, takes issue with their policy advice—both the call for shortening the maturity of the federal debt and for more coordination between the Treasury and the Fed. In contrast, Paul McCulley, formerly at PIMCO and now chairman of the Global Society of Fellows of the Global Interdependence Center in Philadelphia, lauds their recommendations, particularly the need for closely coordinated fiscal and monetary policies when the economy suffers from a liquidity trap, as it did during and following the Great Recession. Stephen G. Cecchetti of Brandeis International Business School endorses some of the authors' analytical observations, but not some of their policy recommendations. And Jason Cummins of asset manager Brevan Howard draws from recent history to illustrate his concerns that too much Fed–Treasury cooperation could pose dangerous risks to the Fed's monetary policy independence.

In chapter 3, John Cochrane of the University of Chicago's Booth School of Business imagines new ways for the U.S. Treasury to borrow, suggesting a variety of novel financial instruments that he argues could reduce the cost to taxpayers of financing federal deficits, provide the liquid and safe securities that markets demand, and manage the interest-rate and other risks that the government and the overall economy face. Cochrane suggests that the government rely heavily on debts with no fixed maturity—perpetuals, in the jargon of the bond trade—that pay interest in a variety of ways, including fixed-value floating-rate debt that resembles shares in money-market mutual funds. Darrell Duffie of Stanford's Graduate School of Business applauds Cochrane's audacity, but challenges the wisdom of the Treasury abandoning the practice of issuing debt of varying maturities.

The book closes with concluding observations from Larry Summers, who has been both a policymaker—as U.S. Treasury secretary and director of the White House National Economic Council—and a professor at Harvard University. "Debt management is too important to leave to debt managers," he argues.

1

THE OPTIMAL MATURITY
OF GOVERNMENT DEBT

Robin Greenwood, Samuel G. Hanson,
Joshua S. Rudolph, and Lawrence H. Summers

The central task of debt management is to decide which debt instruments the government should issue in order to finance itself over time. What programs the government should pursue and whether the government should finance its current expenditures by collecting taxes or by borrowing are outside the purview of debt management.

Historically, U.S. debt managers had three main instruments available to them: Treasury bills with a maturity of less than one year, intermediate-maturity notes with maturities up to ten years, and long-term bonds. Inflation-protected securities were introduced in 1997 and floating-rate notes were added in 2014. The maturity structure of the government debt has fluctuated significantly over time in response to the evolving fiscal outlook and changing debt management practices. The average maturity of Treasury marketable securities outstanding went from sixty-eight months in January 2000 to fifty-five months in January 2007, before the onset of the financial crisis, to sixty-eight months in December 2014.[1]

---

1. See 2015Q1 Quarterly Data Release (www.treasury.gov/resource-center/data-chart-center/quarterly-refunding/Documents/2015%20Q1%20Quarterly%20Data%20Release.xls).

In this chapter we address optimal government debt management policy on a consolidated basis. We begin by describing the considerations the government must weigh in deciding the optimal maturity structure of the debt. We then show how similar considerations can help determine other features of the debt structure, such as the mix between inflation-protected securities and traditional bills, notes, and bonds.

The Optimal Maturity Structure of the Net Consolidated Government Debt

Standard economic theory offers surprisingly little guidance as to how officials should manage the government debt. In the textbook theory of government financing, it is irrelevant whether the government decides to finance itself using debt or taxes, or whether the government borrows using short-term or long-term debt. This surprising view—known as "Ricardian equivalence"—was first postulated by David Ricardo in 1820 and formalized by Robert Barro in 1974. Barro's proposition identifies a set of strict assumptions under which the manner in which the government finances its expenditures using taxes and various types of debt has no effect on household consumption and well-being.[2] Theories of optimal government debt management hinge on failures of one or more of these assumptions.

The strict assumptions underlying Ricardian equivalence proposition are that (1) taxation creates no deadweight losses, (2) government debt is valued by investors solely for its cash flows in different states of the world (i.e., investors do not prize the liquidity of government debt in the same way they value the liquidity of cash or checking deposits), and (3) capital markets are frictionless (Barro 1974).[3] If Ricardian equivalence holds, then not only is

2. Ricardian equivalence is the public finance analog of the Modigliani-Miller (1958) theorem, which states that, under certain strict conditions, the way that a corporation finances itself has no effect on the firm's total value.

3. Formally, the assumption that financial markets are frictionless means that any agent's marginal utility of income must price all assets in the same way. Thus, there cannot be important constraints to participating in financial markets, borrowing constraints, short-selling constraints, agency frictions, or other segmentation that leads agents to assign different values to the same asset. Proofs of Ricardian equivalence also assume that agents have infinite horizons, which is often cited as a reason that Ricardian equivalence may fail. However, lifetimes are long enough that

the maturity structure of the debt economically irrelevant, but deficit-financed spending is also irrelevant.

A simple example illustrates the Ricardian logic. Consider a government with an initial accumulated deficit and no future expenditures that must decide whether to finance its deficit by issuing short- or long-term bonds. If the government finances itself solely through the issuance of short-term debt, then the government will have to raise taxes if short-term interest rates rise. However, the rise in interest rates will leave a household that is lending short-term to the government with a bit more in its bank account. Since the government's sources of funds (taxes and proceeds from issuing new debt) must equal its uses of funds (paying off maturing debt), the gain in the household's bank accounts must *precisely* offset the increase in taxes. As a result, issuing more short-term government debt increases the interest rate exposure of households' future tax liabilities, but has a perfectly offsetting effect on the value of their portfolio of bond holdings. It follows that the government should be completely indifferent between issuing short- or long-term debt. This reflects the fact that, in a Ricardian world, government debts are not a form of net wealth for private actors: they simply reflect the present value of future tax liabilities.

Modern debt management policy hinges on four important real-world deviations from the assumptions underpinning Barro's Ricardian equivalence proposition. First, certain types of government debt are net wealth in the sense that they offer investors a valuable set of "liquidity services" above and beyond their financial cash flows: government debt is a safe store of value that can be quickly converted into cash. For example, short-term Treasury bills provide investors with many of the same liquidity and storage services as cash or bank deposits. As a result, the yields on T-bills appear to embed a significant "liquidity premium"—they are lower than they would be in the absence of these liquidity services. Recognizing these liquidity benefits, the government can improve welfare by issuing short-term debt securities that offer investors these special liquidity services.

Second, debt management can play an important role in managing fiscal risk. A standard rationale for fiscal risk management stems from the insight that taxes influence behavior in the private economy through the effects on incentives. All else equal, society is better off when taxes are low and smooth

---

finite lifetimes cannot account for meaningful failures of Ricardian equivalence (Poterba and Summers 1987).

over time (Barro 1979; Lucas and Stokey 1983). A government that does a lot of short-term borrowing exposes its people to the risk that interest rates change, forcing the government to raise taxes in the future. Going further, a government that does a lot of short-term borrowing may be vulnerable; if there is a widespread and growing fear about a government's inability to service its debts, investors may demand sharply higher interest rates or even to refuse to buy short-term debt in a self-fulfilling panic akin to a bank run. Political economy factors may also play a role because even short-lived shocks to deficit financing may lead to cuts in valuable government programs.[4]

Third, real-world capital markets operate with a variety of frictions not envisioned in the Ricardian benchmark. The most relevant friction is that the marginal holder of long-term government bonds is a specialized fixed-income investor who demands more compensation for bearing interest rate risk than the average taxpayer. This segmentation explains why quantitative easing—the purchase of long-term bonds by the Federal Reserve—can influence the prices of financial assets and can therefore function as a tool for managing aggregate demand. Specifically, shortening the maturity of the net government debt causes specialized fixed-income investors to bear less interest rate risk, and may therefore lower the long-term interest rates relative to short-term rates. Quantitative easing (QE) rests on the belief that such interest rate changes are passed through to private borrowers, helping to stimulate long-term corporate investment, residential construction, and consumer spending.

Fourth, because private financial intermediaries can also create highly liquid short-term debt, debt management policy may be able to promote financial stability by altering the behavior of intermediaries (Pozsar 2011, 2012; Krishnamurthy and Vissing-Jorgensen 2013; Greenwood, Hanson, and Stein 2015). Specifically, by issuing more short-term debt, the government can help satiate the public's demand for liquid short-term debt, reducing the private sector's incentives to issue it. In this way, the government may be able to curb the amount of liquidity transformation in the financial system, limiting the likelihood and severity of future financial crises.

4. For instance, Auerbach and Gale (2009) find that, controlling for the difference between actual and potential GDP, roughly one-quarter of the annual change in the federal deficit from 1984 to 2009 was offset by policy, with changes in outlays accounting for slightly more of the response than changes in revenues.

The framework for government debt management that we develop relies on the four real-world frictions outlined above. We start by exploring the implications of the first two frictions and describe a model developed by Greenwood, Hanson, and Stein (2015). In that model, the government pursues a trade-off between its desire to issue "cheap" securities that provide liquidity services and its desire to manage fiscal risk. This simple trade-off model captures the essence of the traditional debt management problem, as framed by Treasury officials: how to finance the public debt at the lowest cost while being prudent from the perspective of fiscal risk.

After describing this trade-off model of government debt policy, we extend it to consider the two nontraditional goals of debt management suggested previously: promoting financial stability and managing aggregate demand. Although these two policy goals are hardly new, the idea of using debt management policies to pursue them has emerged only in recent years. Because our model already considers a trade-off between competing government objectives, it is well suited for analyzing these nontraditional objectives of debt management.

Our framework suggests that optimal debt management hinges on a set of potentially quantifiable forces. Although a rigorous analysis of this sort is beyond the scope of this chapter, we provide some educated guesses regarding the likely magnitude of the relevant forces, describing how they may vary over time. We argue that over the long run, the optimal maturity structure of government debt may be shorter than the government has entertained historically. We explore this idea by describing a counterfactual financing history of the federal government in which the government relies on a much shorter-term funding mix in the postwar era. We also argue that the optimal maturity structure of debt may vary over time, in a direction that is correlated with the path of monetary policy.

A Trade-Off Model of Government Debt Maturity

We start with the question of the optimal maturity structure of the debt. Greenwood, Hanson, and Stein (2015, hereafter GHS) consider a government that trades off two desires: to issue "cheap" securities and to manage fiscal risk.

This trade-off framework captures the essence of debt management as described by Treasury officials. For instance, in 1998, Assistant Secretary Gary

Gensler emphasized the importance of "achieving the lowest cost financing for taxpayers." At the same time, he noted that "Treasury finances across the yield curve" because "a balanced maturity structure mitigates refunding risks." Ten years later, in 2008, Director of the Office of Debt Management Karthik Ramanathan echoed that sentiment, stating that the primary objective of debt management was to achieve the "lowest cost of financing over time," while emphasizing that it is crucial to "spread debt across maturities to reduce risk."

What does it mean to issue "cheap," or to achieve "the lowest cost financing over time"? It cannot simply mean issuing securities with a low current yield-to-maturity. Why? Short-term rates may be low compared to long-term rates because short-term rates are expected to rise in the future. In this case, issuing short-term debt results in low current interest payments, but will likely lead to higher interest payments in the future. This implies that the government should be indifferent between rolling over short-term debt and issuing long-term debt.

The nature of what ought to count as "low cost" goes beyond adjusting for the expected path of future short-term interest rates. Suppose that capital markets are frictionless—all households assign the same value to all financial assets, but long-term bonds offered a higher expected return than short-term bills because of a risk premium, perhaps because long-term bonds were expected to underperform short-term bills in recessions when the average household is hurting. Should the government try to protect households from this risk by issuing shorter-term securities? No! Such a debt management strategy would simply shift risk between households' bond portfolios and their tax liabilities, but leaves households bearing the same total amount of interest rate risk. In the absence of capital market frictions, issuing more short-term debt wouldn't change a thing.

A role for debt management arises if there is a special, non-risk-based demand for particular types of government securities—that is, if different securities provide different amounts of liquidity services, leading their yields to embed differential liquidity premia.[5] Short-term Treasury bills typically embed a larger liquidity premium than long-term Treasuries because bills

---

5. If all forms of government debt provide the same amount of liquidity services, then Ricardian equivalence fails and the overall quantity of government debt will matter; however, the composition of the debt—that is, debt management policy— would be irrelevant.

provide more of the valuable services offered by traditional money (e.g., tremendous liquidity and absolute safety as a near-term store of value).

However, when Treasury debt managers say they are trying to achieve the lowest cost financing for taxpayers, we sense that they have more in mind than capturing differential liquidity premia. Specifically, it seems that—all else being equal—debt managers might prefer a shorter average maturity for the debt in order to conserve on the "term premium" that compensates long-term bond investors for bearing interest rate risk. Is economizing on the term premium a coherent rationale for shortening the average maturity of the debt? If markets are frictionless and all households assign the same value to long-term bonds, then the answer is a clear "no." However, if markets are segmented and long-term bonds are priced by specialized investors who are more worried about interest rate risk than the typical taxpayer, then the government can make the typical taxpayer better off by borrowing short.[6] Since this same segmented market logic underlies the portfolio balance channel of QE, conserving on the term premium may be a defensible rationale for lowering the average maturity of the debt.[7]

Turning to the other side of the trade-off, the government also seeks to minimize fiscal risk, meaning that the cost of servicing the debt should not be too volatile. Issuing too much short-term debt exposes the government to the possibility that interest rates may rise. The formal justification for fiscal risk management is that government should try to avoid budget risk because this directly leads to volatility in tax rates (GHS). And because the marginal deadweight costs of taxation are increasing with the level of taxes—that is, the costs are *convex*—this generates a desire to smooth taxes over time. The reasons to minimize fiscal risk likely go well beyond any deadweight costs associated with volatile taxes. For example, a very short-term maturity structure might make the government vulnerable to self-fulfilling crises akin to a bank run. Furthermore, one may want to limit budget volatility to avoid

6. If markets are segmented, the expected tax savings from conserving on the term premium demanded by specialized bond investors can more than compensate the typical taxpayer for the additional tax volatility.

7. For instance, in 1993 some of President Clinton's economic advisers argued that it would be desirable to shorten the average maturity of the government debt (Wessel 1993). First, they argued that this would reduce the government's interest bill over time by conserving on term premia. Second, they argued that the reduction in supply would lower term premia via a portfolio balance channel, thereby depressing long-term private borrowing rates.

cutting valuable government programs in the face of temporary negative shocks.

We introduce a simplified version of the model in GHS. Consider a government with an initial accumulated debt (D) and no future expenditures that must finance itself through a combination of short-term bonds, long-term bonds, and taxes. Let S denote the fraction of the debt that is short-term and $1-S$ the fraction that is long-term.

Suppose there is a special demand that makes it cheap to issue short-term debt because short-term debt offers more of the same services as base money: tremendous liquidity and absolute safety as a store of value. It is natural to assume that the demand for these monetary services is downward sloping, so the money-like premium on short-term debt is decreasing in the total amount of short-term debt (SD). We assume that debt managers take the path of short-term interest rates (i.e., conventional monetary policy) as given, but recognize that their issuance decisions may impact the liquidity premium on short-term debt.

On the one hand, this liquidity premium makes the government want to issue more short-term debt. On the other hand, because the government must refinance this short-term debt at an uncertain future interest rate, issuing more short-term debt exposes taxpayers to refinancing risk and makes future taxes more volatile, which is costly. Specifically, a spike in interest rates would lead tax rates to jump. However, in a more general sense, such a shock to the budget might lead to a combination of tax increases and spending cuts, both of which would be painful.

Formally, assume that the liquidity premium on short-term debt is γ, that the deadweight costs of taxation are $\left(\dfrac{\lambda}{2}\right)\tau^2$, and that the variance of short-term interest rates is V_r. If the government finances itself by issuing fraction S of short-term debt and $(1-S)$ of long-term debt, it captures a total money premium benefit of γSD. At the same time, this raises the volatility of taxes, which have costs $\left(\dfrac{\lambda}{2}\right)Var[\tau]=\left(\dfrac{\lambda}{2}\right)D^2V_r(S-S_0)^2$, where S_0 is a small number that reflects the maturity structure that minimizes fiscal risk in isolation. Thus, the optimal fraction of short-term government debt is

$$S^* = S_0 + \frac{1}{\lambda D}\frac{\gamma}{V_r}. \tag{1-1}$$

Absent a liquidity premium on short-term debt ($\gamma = C$), the government immunizes itself against refinancing risk by opting for a long-term maturity structure, setting $S = S_0$.[8] In contrast, if there is a liquidity premium on short-term debt ($\gamma > 0$), the government issues more of it, exposing taxpayers to refinancing risk in the process. The larger the premium, the more aggressively the government relies on short-term debt. More generally, one could associate γ in equation (1-1) with other policy-relevant savings from issuing short-term (e.g., with the component of the term premium that compensates specialized bond investors for bearing greater interest rate risk).

Similarly, when short-term interest rates are less volatile (V_r is low), or when budget volatility is less costly (λ is low), the more aggressively the government seeks to capture the liquidity premium on short-term debt.[9] In the limit, if there were no cost associated with budgetary volatility, then the government should continue to shorten the maturity of the debt until the special demand for short-term debt is satiated. In this limiting case, optimal debt management is a generalization of the Friedman (1960) rule of monetary policy, which says that, absent any costs, the Federal Reserve should expand the monetary base until the demand for money is satiated.

Equation (1-3) suggests that for larger values of accumulated debt, the government should issue longer term, with both sides of the key trade-off pointing in the same direction. First, as the overall debt burden grows, the fiscal costs associated with refinancing risk or the possibility of a debt rollover

8. There is a close analogy between equation (1-3) and the classic result from the theory of portfolio choice. For an investor with a risk aversion of a, the optimal share in a risky asset whose excess returns have mean $E[rx]$ and variance $V[rx]$ is $w = E[rx]/aV[rx]$. Thus, the money premium (γ) in equation (1-3) corresponds to the expected excess return ($E[rx]$), the cost of tax volatility times the level of debt-to-GDP (λD) corresponds to the degree of risk aversion (a), and the variance of short-rate shocks (V_r) corresponds to the variance of excess returns ($V[rx]$).

9. Shortening the maturity structure has three logically distinct effects on household well-being. First, it directly raises household well-being because households derive liquidity services from holding money-like T-bills. Second, it raises the volatility of future taxes, which reduces well-being. Third, it lowers taxes today because selling T-bills that embed a liquidity premium provides the government a form of seigniorage revenue. If raising tax revenue is distortionary, but raising seigniorage revenue is not, this adds another force to those summarized in equation (1-3). However, if raising all forms of government revenue—whether through taxes or seigniorage—is distortionary, this tax-lowering consideration disappears.

crisis loom larger. Second, because the demand for liquidity services is downward sloping, the liquidity premium on short-term debt falls as D rises, further reducing the incentive to tilt toward short-term debt.

Consistent with this trade-off view, since the 1951 Treasury Accord, the United States has tended to extend the maturity of the public debt as the overall debt burden has grown. Figure 1-1 plots the fraction of outstanding debt that is long-term (defined as maturing in more than five years) against the debt-to-GDP ratio from 1952 to 2013. The two series are strongly positively correlated (correlation coefficient of 0.71). This relationship between debt maturity and debt-to-GDP is one of the most direct implications of the trade-off model.[10] It is precisely this view that explains why the Treasury lengthened the maturity of its debt beginning in 2009. The Treasury Borrowing Advisory Committee suggested in November 2009 that "the potential for inflation, higher interest rates, and roll over risk should be of material concern ... lengthening the average maturity of debt from 53 months to 74–90 months was recommended."

How large is the special liquidity premium embedded in short-term T-bills? And why might T-bills provide greater liquidity services than longer-term notes and bonds? Krishnamurthy and Vissing-Jorgensen (2012) argue that all Treasuries have some of the same features as traditional money—namely, liquidity and absolute safety. They find that the liquidity services associated with these special attributes lead Treasuries to have significantly lower yields than they otherwise would. Their estimate of the liquidity premium on Treasuries from 1926 to 2008 is seventy-three basis points.[11] However, Krishnamurthy and Vissing-Jorgensen suggest that short- and long-term Treasuries offer very different types of safety, and so are unlikely to be perfect substitutes. T-bills provide short-term safety: the absolute stability of near-term market value. While long-term Treasuries offer long-term safety in the sense of absolute certainty of repayment, they are nevertheless subject to interim market risk. Consistent with the existence of a special demand for

10. The strong relationship between government debt maturity and debt-to-GDP is also noted by Greenwood, Hanson, and Stein (2010); Krishnamurthy and Vissing-Jorgensen (2012); and Greenwood and Vayanos (2014).

11. Krishnamurthy and Vissing-Jorgensen's estimate is based on measuring the impact of changes in Treasury supply on a variety of yield spreads. For example, they show that an increase in Treasury supply reduces the spread between long-term Treasuries and AAA-rated corporate bonds and the spread between short-term Treasury bills and highly rated commercial paper.

FIGURE 1-1. Maturity Structure of the Public Debt and Debt/GDP[a]

Percent

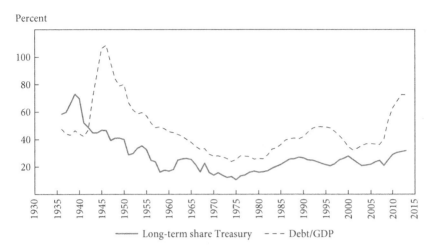

——— Long-term share Treasury   – – – Debt/GDP

Sources: Data were compiled from various issues of the Monthly Statement of the Public Debt, *Treasury Bulletin*, Banking and Monetary Statistics, and *Federal Reserve Bulletin*.

a. The solid line shows the percentage of Treasury debt that has a remaining maturity of five years or more. The dashed line shows the debt-to-GDP ratio.

short-term safety, the yields on short-term T-bills are often quite low relative to those on longer-term notes and bonds (Amihud and Mendelson 1991; Duffee 1996). GHS confirm this by comparing actual T-bill yields with "fitted yields," where the fitted yield is an estimate of what the yields on T-bills should be, based on the shape of the rest of the yield curve. Their analysis suggests that on average, from 1983 to 2009 four-week bills had yields roughly forty basis points *below* their fitted values based on longer-term Treasuries.

Figure 1-2 illustrates the special money-like premium on very short-term Treasury bills. Panel A plots the yield on one-month T-bills versus the one-month overnight index swap (OIS) rate, which is a good proxy for the default-free short-term rate that does not benefit from these special liquidity premia.[12]

12. The OIS rate is unlikely to be affected by default risk since it is based on the expected overnight Federal funds rate. And it is largely free of any convenience premium since it is not a rate at which a money-market investor can invest principal (i.e., a swap is not a stable-value store of value in the same way as a T-bill or financial CP).

FIGURE 1-2. Estimates of Liquidity Premia on Treasuries

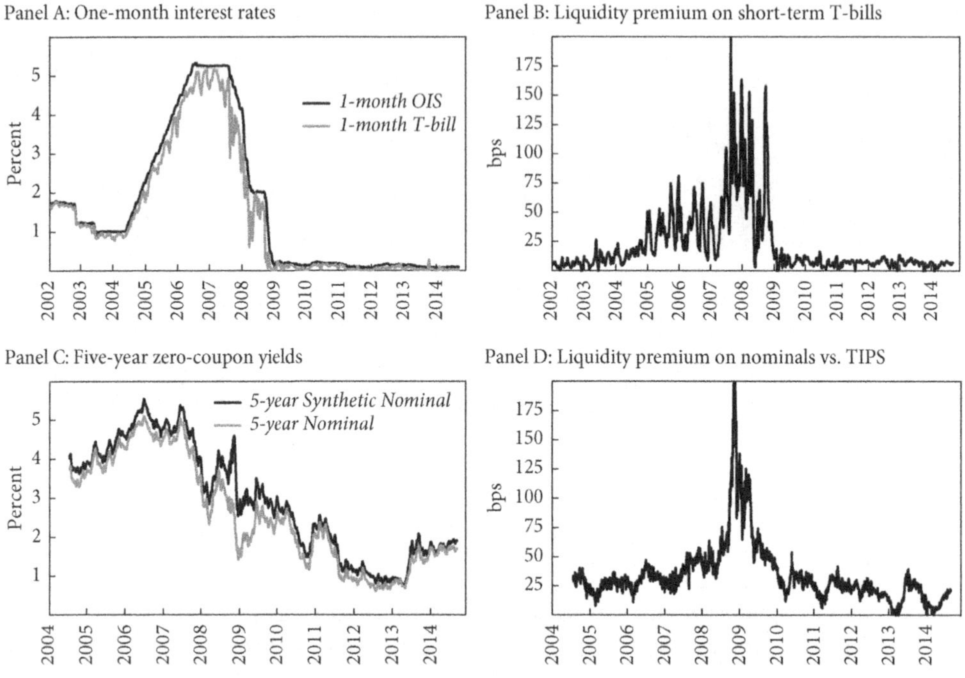

Panel A: One-month interest rates

Panel B: Liquidity premium on short-term T-bills

Panel C: Five-year zero-coupon yields

Panel D: Liquidity premium on nominals vs. TIPS

Sources: Federal Reserve Economic Database; Bloomberg; Zero-coupon nominal Treasury and TIPS yields are from Gurkaynak, Sack, and Wright (2007, 2010).

Note: Panel A plots the yield on one-month Treasury bills from the Federal Reserve Economic Database (FRED) and the one-month overnight index swap (OIS) rate from Bloomberg. Panel B plots the difference between the one-month OIS rate and the one-month T-bill rate. Panel C plots the yield on a *synthetic* five-year zero-coupon nominal Treasury—computed as the sum of the five-year TIPS yield at the five-year inflation swap yield—versus the actual five-year zero-coupon yield for nominal Treasuries. Panel D plots the difference between the synthetic nominal yield and the actual nominal yield. In all four panels, we show the weekly moving averages of daily data.

Panel B plots the spread between the one-month OIS rate and the one-month T-bill rate. This spread reflects the special money-like liquidity premium on T-bills. GHS show that these convenience premia are particularly pronounced for very short-term bills such as those maturing in less than a quarter or a month.

There is strong evidence that shifts in these liquidity premia are driven by shifts in the demand and supply of money-like assets. Specifically, Krishnamurthy and Vissing-Jorgensen (2012) and GHS find that shifts in T-bill supply due to movements in the debt-to-GDP ratio can explain much of the low-frequency variation in the liquidity premia on T-bills. Nagel (2014) argues that shifts in the demand for money-like debt associated with changes in the level of short-term nominal interest rates explain much of the business-cycle frequency variation in these premia. Specifically, demand for money-like debt and hence liquidity premia are high when short-term interest rates are high. This pattern is clearly evident even in the short time-series shown in Figure 1-2.[13] At higher frequencies, the variation in these spreads is explained as seasonal fluctuations in T-bill supply (GHS) and week-to-week shifts in the institutional demand for money market investments, as well as flight-to-quality episodes (Sunderam 2014).

How large are the fiscal risk costs associated with issuing more short-term debt? In the GHS model, fiscal costs coming from the deadweight costs of taxation are $\left(\dfrac{\lambda}{2}\right)\tau^2$, so the marginal deadweight cost is $\lambda\tau$. A conservative upper bound on the marginal deadweight cost is 0.5 (Chetty 2012). Assuming a tax rate of roughly 25 percent, this implies an upper bound of $\lambda = z$. Thus, the costs of distortionary taxation are no greater than $E[\tau]^2 = (E[\tau])^2 + Var[\tau]$. Assuming $E[\tau] = 25$ percent, this implies that $E[\tau]^2 = 6.25$ percent. However, the component of $Var[\tau]$ driven by fluctuations in interest rates is likely an order of magnitude smaller. In other words, plausible estimates of the welfare costs from the failure to smooth taxes over time are tiny.

Although emphasized by GHS in their formal model, thinking of fiscal risk as solely the distortionary costs of taxation is too limited. Consider the following back-of-the-envelope calculation. Suppose all the debt is short-term

13. Nagel's (2014) argument is that short-term debt is a partial substitute for traditional forms of money such as currency and checking deposits. Since traditional money pays little or no interest, the nominal interest rate is the opportunity cost of holding money. Similarly, the liquidity premium—that is, the difference between the yield on an illiquid short-term deposit and the yield on liquid short-term debt— is the opportunity cost of holding money-like short-term debt. All else equal, this suggests that savers will want to hold less traditional money and more money-like short-term debt when short-term interest rates rise. Consistent with this view, savings tend to flow out of non-interest-bearing checking accounts and into money-market funds when short-term interest rates are high.

and is refinanced once each year. Then, at the current debt-to-GDP ratio of 70 percent, a 1 percentage point increase in short-term real interest rates raises the ratio of interest expense to GDP by 0.70 percent, or $120 billion, based on 2014Q2 GDP of $17.3 trillion (at an annual rate). This is not a trivial shock to the federal budget, exceeding the projected 2014 outlays of the Departments of Homeland Security ($50 billion), Education ($65 billion), Labor ($75 billion), and Transportation ($80 billion). An unlikely 5 percentage point increase in short-term real rates would raise interest costs by 3.5 percent of GDP, or by $600 billion, exceeding the projected 2014 outlays for the Department of Defense ($595 billion). Calculations of this sort have often been used to motivate a strategy of extending the maturity of the debt (Cochrane, chapter 3 of this book).

Common sense suggests that the government might be willing to pay some insurance premium to avoid such scenarios. For instance, suppose we pay an additional 0.20 percent in interest on the debt to keep the interest expense smooth. In dollar terms, an annual premium of $25 billion (= $17.3 trillion × 70% × 0.20%) could insure against potential budgetary shocks of the magnitude described.

However, even if the government is willing to pay *some* insurance premium to reduce fiscal risk, there are two important reasons to think that the government may be able to take advantage of the large liquidity premium on short-term bills without incurring much additional risk. First, substituting one-month T-bills, for which liquidity premia are very high, for six-month T-bills may allow the government to capture the liquidity premium without significantly increasing overall budget volatility. This is because both one-month and six-month bills are similar from the perspective of interest rate risk.

Second, issuing short-term debt may be a natural hedge for fiscal shocks to the primary budget deficit. Specifically, the only source of fiscal risk in the baseline GHS model is due to uncertainty about the path of future short-term interest rates. However, debt managers also deal with volatility from the budgeting process that increases the overall debt burden. Consider the case where government debt managers are uncertain about both the path of future short-term interest rates as well as future primary fiscal deficits. In this regard, the existence of automatic stabilizers—the fact that government tax proceeds tend to fall and transfer payments tend to rise in recessions—suggests that primary fiscal deficits will tend to be high during recessions when short-term interest rates are low. This adds an additional fiscal hedging motive for issuing short-term debt. The idea is that the cost of refinancing short-term debt tends to be low in states when primary deficits are high. Specifically, adapting the baseline GHS model, it is straightforward to show that the optimal fraction of short-term government debt is

$$S^* = S_0 + \frac{1}{\lambda D} \frac{\gamma}{V_r} - \frac{\beta_{G,r}}{D}, \tag{1-2}$$

where $\beta_{G,r}$ is the coefficient from a regression of unexpected future government deficits (G) on short-term real rates (r).[14] Since we expect $\beta_{G,r} < 0$, this fiscal hedging motive should push the government to adopt even more short-term debt maturity structure.

Debt Management and Aggregate Demand

Policymakers have tended to see monetary policy as distinct from debt management. However, the clean lines of demarcation between these branches of policy have been blurred since 2008. The Fed's quantitative easing policies, which have swapped long-term Treasuries for short-term interest-bearing reserves, have shortened the maturity of the net consolidated debt held by the public.[15] Fed officials have argued that shortening the maturity of the consolidated public debt should lower the general level of long-term interest rates relative to short-term rates, stimulating long-term investment and consumption. In other words, the maturity structure of the public debt may be a tool of aggregate demand management. This may be one of the only tools available to the Fed for combating high unemployment and the threat of price deflation once nominal interest rates hit zero.

Holding fixed the path of short-term interest rates and the total size of the debt, how can the average maturity of government debt affect long-term

---

14. Equation (1-4) follows from the observation that with an unknown future deficit of G, we have $\left(\frac{\lambda}{2}\right) Var[\tau] = \left(\frac{\lambda}{2}\right)[V_r D^2 (S - S_0)^2 + V_G + 2D(S - S_0)C_{G,r}]$, where $V_G = Var[G]$ and $C_{G,r} = Cov[G, r]$.

15. Technically, QE can be thought of as combination of a "conventional monetary easing," in which the Fed expands the supply of bank reserves by purchasing T-bills, and an Operation Twist, in which the Fed sells T-bills and buys long-term Treasuries. The conventional easing component has no effect at the zero lower bound, so the entire effect must come from the Operation Twist component (Woodford 2012).

interest rates? The idea is that a reduction in government debt maturity lowers the amount of interest rate risk that fixed-income investors have to bear, leading to a decline in the term premium—that is, the difference in expected returns between long- and short-term bonds—due to a Tobin-style portfolio balance effect (Tobin 1958). Thus, the relevant summary statistic for such portfolio balance policies would be the weighted average (or total dollar) duration held by private, fixed-income investors.[16]

The strong evidence that debt management policies do impact term premia suggests that interest rate risk that is borne by investors directly through bond markets looms larger than interest rate risk that is borne indirectly by taxpayers.[17] As noted, the most natural explanation for this non-Ricardian result is that the marginal investor in bonds is a specialized, fixed-income investor who is far more heavily exposed to interest rate risk than the typical taxpayer. Thus, a reduction in the duration of government debt only succeeds in lowering term premia because it asks the typical taxpayer to bear a tiny bit more interest rate risk so that the marginal bond investor can bear much less risk (Woodford 2012; Greenwood and Vayanos 2014; Hanson 2014).

Debt Management as a Financial Regulatory Tool

Financial regulation and debt management have historically been seen as separate spheres of policy. However, the desire to promote a stable financial system may push the government further toward a shorter-term maturity structure (GHS).

To understand the argument, note that the government is not the only entity that can create riskless money-like short-term debt. Specifically, Gorton (2010), Pozsar (2011, 2012), Gorton and Metrick (2012), Stein (2012), and

---

16. In the formulation of this idea by Vayanos and Vila (2009) and Greenwood and Vayanos (2014), term premia are proportional to the product of interest rate risk and dollar duration, scaled by the risk tolerance of bond investors.

17. See Greenwood and Vayanos (2014) for comprehensive evidence from the postwar era. See also Gagnon and others (2011), Krishnamurthy and Vissing-Jorgensen (2011), Jarrow and Li (2012), and Li and Wei (2013) for appraisals of the Fed's large-scale asset purchase programs. See Bernanke, Reinhart, and Sack (2004); Greenwood and Vayanos (2010); and Swanson (2011) for event study evidence predating the LSAPS. Relatedly, Hanson (2014) and Malkhozov and others (2014) provide strong evidence that shifts in the duration of U.S. mortgage-backed securities move bond term premia, even though they would have no effect if markets were frictionless.

Krishnamurthy and Vissing-Jorgensen (2013) argue that when financial intermediaries issue money-like short-term debt that is collateralized by long-term risky assets, they are engaged in liquidity creation. In this way, they capture some of the same liquidity premium as the Treasury does when it issues T-bills. While some amount of private liquidity transformation is desirable, the incentives for private liquidity creation are likely excessive because individual intermediaries do not take into account the full financial stability costs that are generated by their use of short-term funding. Put differently, liquidity transformation generates negative externalities, so government policies that work to reduce intermediaries' overreliance on short-term funding may be desirable. And private liquidity transformation may be hard to regulate, particularly if it is done by the shadow banking sector.

What role can the government play through debt management? The government may "crowd out" some private sector short-term issuance by issuing more of its own short-term debt. An expansion in the supply of Treasury bills would lower the premium on short-term money-like debt and reduce the temptation for private intermediaries to issue short.[18] Of course, this policy response is not without cost since it generates additional fiscal risk. Thus, it is not optimal for the government to issue so much short-term debt as to completely counteract intermediaries' tendency to overrely on short-term funding. Said differently, the government should keep shortening its maturity as long as it has a comparative advantage over the private sector in the production of money-like short-term debt.

Another way to address the financial stability externalities associated with private liquidity transformation would be to regulate short-term private liabilities (Ricks 2013; Cochrane 2014). Private liquidity transformation could be directly controlled using a regulatory cap, as under the Basel III bank liquidity regulations, or by taxing short-term issuance directly, as suggested by Kashyap and Stein (2012) and Stein (2012). However, to the extent that direct regulation simply pushes liquidity transformation into the unregulated shadows, there will be a complementary role for a debt management policy. Specifically, by influencing the liquidity premium on short-term debt, debt management can influence private sector incentives to engage in liquidity transformation, reaching into corners of the financial markets that lie beyond

---

18. See GHS, Krishnamurthy and Vissing-Jorgensen (2013), Carlson and others (2014), and Sunderam (2014) for evidence that a rise in short-term government debt crowds out short-term debt issuance by financial intermediaries.

the grasp of regulators. In other words, the advantage of debt management over direct regulation is that it "gets in all the cracks" (Stein 2013).

GHS argue that this crowding-out motive for issuing short-term T-bills may be of the same order of magnitude as the direct motive for producing debt with the liquidity services highlighted previously. Thus, when weighed against the fiscal risk costs of issuing additional short-term debt, this financial stability benefit may be sufficient to meaningfully shorten the optimal maturity structure of the government debt.

Quantitative Assessment and Debt Counterfactuals

The analysis thus far suggests that the forces in favor of short-term debt appear to be larger than conventionally thought. Still, this does not provide much quantitative guidance as to whether the weighted average maturity of the debt should be 12 months, 60 months, or 120 months. In this section, we take a simple approach to this question by describing the results of a counterfactual exercise in which we suppose that the government had relied much more heavily on short-term debt following the 1951 Accord.

We focus on the extreme case in which the government had financed the debt using three-month T-bills, meaning that the entire outstanding debt would be refinanced four times per year. We start by noting that the change in the debt equals the primary deficit (outlays and net transfer payments minus total tax revenue) plus interest paid:

$$\text{Debt}_t = \text{Debt}_{t-1} + \text{PrimDef}_t + \text{Interest}_t, \tag{1-3}$$

where Debt_t refers to the public debt held at the end of the fiscal year t (including debt held by the Federal Reserve), PrimDef_t refers to the primary deficit, and Interest_t refers to interest paid, including coupons on notes and bonds and imputed interest on Treasury bills that do not pay a coupon. We obtain Debt_t and Interest_t from the Office of Management and Budget, and use this data to back out the primary deficit according to equation (1-3). Our data start in June 30, 1951 (start of the 1952 fiscal year), capturing the start of the post-Accord period.

Figure 1-3 shows the time-series of average interest payments, expressed as a percentage of GDP. Interest payments average 1.8 percent of GDP per year, reflecting an average effective nominal interest rate paid of 4.97 percent.

$\dfrac{\text{Interest}}{\text{GDP}}$ is quite smooth over time, with a standard deviation of only 0.72 percent. In part, this reflects the average long-term nature of the debt and the fact that debt-to-GDP has been moderate over much of this 1952–2013 sample.

Our counterfactual exercise assumes a debt management strategy of continuously rolling over three-month Treasury bills. We assume that the actual short-term interest rates that have prevailed since 1952 would have also prevailed under this counterfactual strategy. In doing so, we ignore the fact that the path of short-term interest rates would likely have been slightly different due to the deviations from Ricardian equivalence. For instance, in the extreme, financing the government entirely with short-term bills might make the government susceptible to bank-run-like outcomes, which could have a significant impact on interest rates.

We compute the effective annual interest rate under this counterfactual debt management policy, $R^{\text{Counterfactual}}$, by compounding three-month Treasury bill rates.[19] We then compute counterfactual interest payments according to

$$\text{Interest}_t^{\text{Counterfactual}} = \text{Debt}_{t-1}^{\text{Counterfactual}} \times R_t^{\text{Counterfactual}}. \qquad (1\text{-}4)$$

Modifying equation (1-4) allows us to compute a counterfactual evolution of the debt stock as

$$\text{Debt}_t^{\text{Counterfactual}} = \text{Debt}_{t-1}^{\text{Counterfactual}} + \text{PrimDef}_t + \text{Interest}_t^{\text{Counterfactual}}. \qquad (1\text{-}5)$$

Thus, starting with the actual debt outstanding at the end of 1951, we can construct a counterfactual path for $\dfrac{\text{Interest}}{\text{GDP}}$ and $\dfrac{\text{Debt}}{\text{GDP}}$, taking as given the government's realized primary deficits.

---

19. We obtain month-end data on three-month T-bill rates from the Federal Reserve Bank of St. Louis's FRED database. To compute the interest paid on a fiscal year basis (the federal government's fiscal year runs from October 1 to September 30), we compute the effective annual rate as $R^{\text{Counterfactual}} = [(1+r_{(\text{Sept.})})(1+r_{(\text{Dec.})}) \times (1+r_{(\text{March})})(1+r_{(\text{June})})]^{\frac{1}{4}} - 1$, where the subscripts on the three-month T-bill rate indicate the relevant month-end.

FIGURE 1-3. Debt and Deficits under Counterfactual Debt Management Plans

Panel A: Actual and counterfactual interest payments and primary balance
Percent GDP

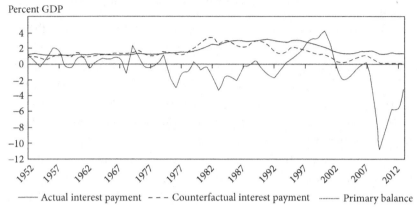

——— Actual interest payment   - - - Counterfactual interest payment   ········ Primary balance

Panel B: Total surplus in actual data and counterfactual
Percent GDP

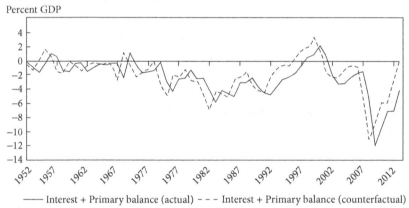

——— Interest + Primary balance (actual)   - - - Interest + Primary balance (counterfactual)

Panel C: Debt and counterfactual debt burden
Percent GDP

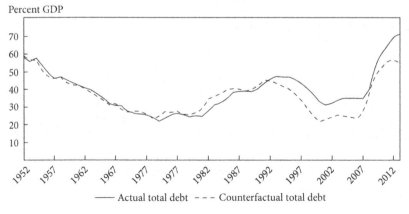

——— Actual total debt   - - - Counterfactual total debt

FIGURE 1-3. *Continued*

Sources: Office of Management and Budget; Federal Reserve Economic Database; Authors' calculations.

Note: The counterfactual exercise measures the path of deficits and debt supposing that the U.S. Treasury had financed itself using rolling three-month Treasury bills starting in 1952. We use the identity, $\text{Debt}_t = \text{Debt}_{t-1} + \text{PrimDef}_t + \text{Interest}_t$, and data on debt and net interest payments to back out primary deficits. Debt held by the public is from the Office of Management and Budget (OMB); net interest expense is also from the OMB. In the counterfactual case, starting in September 1952, we compute net interest as the compounded interest from rolling over three-month Treasury bills over the government fiscal year. Panel A shows actual and counterfactual interest payments, scaled by GDP. For purposes of comparison, it also shows the path of primary surpluses and deficits (surpluses carry a positive sign). In Panel B we combined interest payments and the primary balance to show the combined total surplus, in both the actual data and the counterfactual. In Panel C we show the debt burden, as a percentage of GDP, in the realized and counterfactual cases.

Figure 1-3 shows that issuing short-term debt results in higher volatility of interest payments. The volatility of $\dfrac{\text{Interest}}{\text{GDP}}$ is 0.84 percent under the counterfactual strategy, compared to 0.72 percent under the actual strategy. How should we evaluate these numbers? Panel A in figure 1-3 shows that the volatility of $\dfrac{\text{Interest}}{\text{GDP}}$ —whether in the actual or counterfactual case—is quite small compared to the volatility in $\dfrac{\text{PrimDef}}{\text{GDP}}$, which has an annual time-series volatility of 2.54 percent. But a simple comparison of the time-series volatilities under different financing regimes does not suffice, because the net increase in the debt stock is the *sum* of interest payments and the primary deficit, meaning that a short-term financing policy can serve as a hedge against primary deficits. The simple explanation is that the primary deficit tends to be larger when the economy is performing poorly and is associated with low or declining short-term interest rates.

How much did the government save in this counterfactual financing strategy? Our calculations suggest the government would have saved 0.38 percentage points of GDP per year. Panel C in figure 1-3 shows that the cumulative interest savings would have meaningfully lowered the debt stock over time. By the end of the sample, the public debt was 71.3 percent of GDP, whereas in the counterfactual case, it was only 54.8 percent.

What this makes clear is that *ex post*, the government would have been better off financing its debt over the short-term. To be clear, we are not suggesting that we should use this exercise as an estimate of the interest cost savings that would be obtained by shortening the maturity of the debt going forward. For one thing, in the 1980s, the United States experienced a decline in inflation that was unexpected by market participants, a situation unlikely to be repeated. Notwithstanding, figure 1-3 shows estimated *ex ante* term premia as estimated by Kim and Wright (2005), which averaged forty-five basis points per annum on five-year zero-coupon debt from 1989 to 2013. Second, the logic of our model suggests that the average savings we computed overstates the welfare benefits from adopting a shorter debt maturity profile. The reason is that some of the term premium on long-term bond is surely compensation for risk in the traditional frictionless, asset-pricing sense. However, the government is not making households any better off by issuing short-term to "economize" on this risk premium since this necessarily increases the interest rate exposure of household's tax liabilities. Only the component of the term premium that is due to the T-bills providing higher liquidity convenience services or stemming from segmented bond markets should count from a welfare perspective.[20]

In summary, the main messages we take from these counterfactual exercises are (1) that the additional budgetary volatility incurred by shifting the government debt into short-term securities is less than is commonly supposed, and (2) that doing this would have allowed the government to capture liquidity premia on an ongoing basis.

---

20. We have repeated this counterfactual exercise in real terms, meaning that we compute the real value of the debt and the real interest (both as it happened and in the counterfactual case in which the government rolled over short-term debt). Expressed in real terms, the "interest burden" of the debt reflects a combination of shocks to real interest rates and inflation. Real interest payments are more volatile than nominal interest payments. The standard deviation in the counterfactual case is 1.97 percent, more than twice the standard deviation of actual interest paid (0.81 percent). Both series are still less volatile than real primary deficits, which have a standard deviation of 2.52 percent. The correlation between the real actual interest payment and the real primary deficit is not significantly different from zero. In the counterfactual case, however, the correlation between effective real interest payments and the primary deficit is –0.39. This can be compared to the –0.26 correlation between nominal interest payments and the nominal primary deficit.

Debt Management beyond Maturity Structure

The framework for debt management that we have developed here can be extended to accommodate a host of issues beyond the question of the optimal maturity structure. We briefly discuss these extensions here.

The Choice of Nominal versus Inflation-Indexed Debt

Consider for example the choice between long-term nominal and inflation-indexed debt. To do so, we need to distinguish between shocks to real interest rates and the rate of inflation. The government can now issue short-term bonds (automatically inflation-indexed since we assume that uncertainty about inflation is minimal at short horizons), long-term nominal bonds, and long-term inflation-indexed bonds.

Suppose that government debt managers take the path of inflation and short-term real rates as given. If short-term real interest rates tend to be high when inflation is high—as one would expect if the Federal Reserve follows a standard Taylor rule—then short-term debt and long-term nominal debt will be complementary from a fiscal risk perspective. Suppose, for example, that inflation is low so that the real tax burden needed to service long-term nominal debt is high. Since short-term real rates are likely to be low in such a state, this makes short-term debt a good hedge for long-term nominal debt.

Beyond these risk management considerations, there is strong evidence that long-term nominal Treasuries embed a significant liquidity premium relative to long-term Treasury inflation-protected securities (TIPS) (Campbell, Shiller, and Viceira 2009; Fleckenstein, Longstaff, and Lustig 2014; Pflueger and Viceira 2013).

How large is the premium on nominal versus inflation-indexed debt? Fleckenstein, Longstaff, and Lustig (2014) estimate an average liquidity premium of roughly fifty-five basis points on nominal Treasuries compared to TIPS from 2004 to 2009.[21] Pflueger and Viceira (2013) find similar magnitudes for the United States, as well as from inflation-indexed debt in the United Kingdom. Both papers argue that this is not simply the capitalized value of

---

21. Fleckenstein, Longstaff, and Lustig (2014) show that the price of nominal Treasury bonds exceeds the price of a portfolio consisting of a maturity-matched TIPS and an inflation swap that replicates the cash flows on the nominal Treasury. This implies that the yields on nominal Treasuries are lower because of a liquidity premium.

future bid-ask spreads or other transaction costs. Instead, it appears to reflect a special liquidity premium.

In figure 1-2, we show an estimate of the liquidity premium on nominal bonds from 2004 to 2014. Specifically, our estimate of the nominal liquidity premium is the yield on five-year TIPS, plus the yield on a five-year inflation swap, minus the yield on a five-year nominal Treasury note. Since an investor can generate the exact same financial cash flows by buying a five-year nominal Treasury or by buying a five-year TIPS note and entering into an inflation swap (receiving the swap yield and paying realized inflation), this spread should be zero if investors derived the same liquidity services from holding nominal and inflation-indexed debt. By contrast, this spread will be positive if investors derive greater liquidity services from holding nominal debt. As shown in panel D of figure 1-2, the liquidity premium on nominal Treasuries versus TIPS spiked during the financial crisis and has averaged roughly 35 bps from 2004 to 2014.

Formally, let S be the fraction of debt that is short-term and N be the fraction of debt that is long-term and nominal. The remaining $1-S-N$ of the debt will be long-term and inflation-indexed. Let $1-S-N$ be the liquidity premium on long-term nominal debt and $\gamma \geq 0$ be the premium on short-term debt, both measured relative to long-term TIPS. Extending the logic in GHS, the optimal debt portfolio is given by

$$S = \frac{1}{2} + \frac{1}{\lambda D}\frac{\gamma}{V_r}\frac{1}{1-R_{r,\pi}^2} + \frac{1}{\lambda D}\frac{\theta}{V_r}\frac{\beta_{r,\pi}}{1-R_{r,\pi}^2} \tag{1-6a}$$

$$N = \frac{1}{\lambda D}\frac{\theta}{V_\pi}\frac{1}{1-R_{r,\pi}^2} + \frac{1}{\lambda D}\frac{\gamma}{V_\pi}\frac{\beta_{\pi,r}}{1-R_{r,\pi}^2}, \tag{1-6b}$$

where V_π is the variance of inflation, $\beta_{r,\pi}$ is the coefficient from a regression of short-term real rates on inflation, $\beta_{\pi,r}$ is the coefficient from the reverse regression of inflation on real rates, and $R_{r,\pi}^2$ is the goodness of fit from these regressions.[22]

---

22. Equations (1-6a) and (1-6b) follow from the observation that with an unknown future inflation of π, we have $\left(\frac{\lambda}{2}\right)Var[\tau] = \left(\frac{\lambda}{2}\right)D^2[V_r(S-S_0)^2 + V_\pi N^2 - 2(S-S_0)NC_{\pi,r}]$, where $V_\pi = Var[\pi]$ and $C_{\pi,r} = Cov[\pi, r]$.

To interpret equations (1-6a) and (1-6b), note that if $\gamma = \theta = 0$, the government should not issue long-term nominal debt since doing so only raises the variability of the tax burden in real terms. This is consistent with Summers (1997), who summarized the rationale for introducing TIPS in 1997 as: "We were attracted to them by their ability to stabilize debt payments by the government."

Next, if shocks to short-term real rates and inflation are uncorrelated (so $\beta_{r,\pi} = \beta_{\pi,r} = R_{r,\pi}^2 = 0$), the optimal short-term share S depends on the premium on short-term debt (γ) and is limited by the volatility of short-term real rates (V_r), and the optimal share of long-term nominal debt depends on the premium on nominal debt (θ) and is limited by the volatility of inflation (V_r). Finally, in the plausible case where inflation and real rates are positively correlated, equations (1-6a) and (1-6b) capture the complementarity of short and nominal debt from a fiscal risk perspective. For instance, the tendency to issue short and nominal debt is largest when the R^2 from a regression of real rates on inflation is high. In this case, short-term debt is a good hedge for nominal debt and vice versa, so the government can be quite aggressive in catering to the special liquidity demands for short-term debt and long-term nominal debt without incurring significant tax-smoothing costs.

We have assumed that government debt managers take the inflation process as given. While this strikes us as an accurate description of the situation today and in most of the postwar era, this may not be true in situations where the debt burden becomes extreme. By relying on nominal debt, the government may be able to smooth the real tax burden by engineering a large inflation following the accumulation of significant fiscal deficits. This safety valve may make long-term nominal debt more desirable than inflation-indexed debt. Looking across history, Reinhart and Sbrancia (2011) and Piketty (2014) describe how the accumulation of massive government deficits during major wars has often been followed by inflationary episodes that have significantly reduced the debt burden in real terms.[23] Ferguson, Schaab, and Schularick

---

23. This regularity is linked to the fiscal theory of the price level (Leeper 1991; Sims 1994; Woodford 1995; Cochrane 2001). This theory says that if a government has an unsustainable fiscal policy, such that it will not be able to repay its debts out of future primary surpluses, then it will choose to inflate away the debt. Thus, the current nominal price level is pinned down by the current level of nominal

(2014) suggest that periods of central bank balance sheet growth have been undone mostly via inflation rather than nominal declines.

Additional Considerations

Our framework can easily be extended to incorporate additional debt management considerations. Two additional considerations stand out.

First, Treasury officials routinely argue that debt management policies play a role in promoting the infrastructure and broader efficiency of U.S. capital markets. Specifically, it is arguably useful to investors in other fixed-income assets—including corporate bonds, municipal bonds, mortgage-backed securities, and asset-backed securities—to have liquid benchmark Treasury securities with maturities of, say, two, five, ten, and thirty years. Such transparent benchmarks for the risk-free rate may facilitate new issue pricing in other markets and may also be useful for hedging (Fleming 2000). The desire to maintain liquid benchmark Treasury issues became an increasing concern in the late 1990s when the government ran a series of large fiscal surpluses and was expected to significantly pay down the debt over time. Indeed, one of the major rationales for the Treasury's 2000–2001 buyback operations was to maintain large five-, ten-, and thirty-year on-the-run benchmark issues in an era of declining overall debt supply (Sachs 1999; Fleming 2000). Several sovereigns, including Chile, have opted to maintain a liquid benchmark yield curve even when total debt was near zero.[24]

Promoting financial market infrastructure by issuing liquid benchmark securities can be viewed as a kind of nonpecuniary service generated by government debt. However, some of the "benchmark" value of Treasuries has a public good character and thus is unlikely to be fully captured in the market prices.

Second, we have discussed the liquidity premia on short-term government debt and nominal government debt and explained why the government should cater to these special demands. However, there may be other

---

government debt and the expected value of future real primary surpluses. In this way, fiscal discipline is a critical necessary condition for price stability.

24. Since 2003, the Chilean government has regularly issued domestic bonds despite being in a net creditor position. The stated aim of these issuances is to enhance bond market liquidity in Chile.

government securities that embed significant liquidity premia. For example, "on-the-run" Treasuries typically embed a liquidity premium relative to "off-the-run" issues with nearly identical cash flows (Warga 1992; Krishnamurthy 2002; Vayanos and Weill 2008). This makes them especially useful for risk management and hedging.

Debt-buyback operations, such as those undertaken from 2000 to 2001, can be understood as a case where issuing securities with a greater liquidity premium imposes little, if any, additional fiscal risk for the government. Specifically, if there is a special liquidity premium on "on the run" Treasury securities (e.g., the on-the-run thirty-year bond), then the government can engage in a form of liquidity creation that entails little, if any, fiscal risk by issuing thirty-year bonds that command a large convenience premium and repurchasing these bonds when they become twenty-nine-year bonds with a much smaller convenience premium (Garbade and Rutherford 2007).

Summary

Optimal debt management hinges on trade-offs between four potentially competing objectives: (1) financing the government at least cost by catering to liquidity premia and economizing on term premia; (2) limiting fiscal risk, particularly that associated with short-term financing; (3) managing aggregate demand by using the maturity of government debt to influence long-term interest rates; and (4) promoting financial stability by issuing enough short-term government debt to counteract the financial system's tendency toward excessive liquidity transformation.

Many of these forces can be readily quantified. For example, researchers have developed a variety of methods to estimate liquidity premia and term premia. And the recent experience of the Federal Reserve and other central banks with quantitative easing policies have provided researchers with an increasing amount of data to assess the aggregate demand effects of debt management policy.

However, some of these forces are more difficult to quantify and require further study. For example, researchers have only begun to examine the financial stability benefits that may accrue when the government issues more short-term debt. Similarly, while it is possible to project the budgetary consequences of different debt management policies, it is less clear how to assess the ultimate cost of budgetary volatility.

COMMENT

Janice Eberly

Greenwood, Hanson, Rudolph, and Summers bring together academic research, practical experience in policy, and empirical observation to inform debt management, in particular the maturity structure of debt, in concert with monetary policy. Undertaking this project recognizes the singular position of monetary and fiscal policy during and after the global financial crisis of 2008–09. Monetary policy in the United States and elsewhere went to extraordinary lengths to support markets and the economy, driving the policy rate to zero and then directly transacting in asset markets through quantitative easing. While fiscal policy also undertook extraordinary measures, this chapter addresses an often-undervalued component of fiscal policy: the issuance of the debt that finances a fiscal deficit. While often seen as passive or at most technocratic, in a financial crisis the maturity structure of the available debt may itself be a policy instrument. In fact, if quantitative easing affects the real economy through the demand for Treasury assets, then the maturity structure of Treasury issuance must also affect the real economy through the supply of those same assets. In other words, an alternative to quantitative easing may be to issue fewer longer-term Treasuries in the first place, a point on which the authors elaborate in chapter 2.

Before addressing the substantive points made here, it is worth remarking on the methodology, which threads the needle between academic methods of empirical analysis and modeling, together with a practical policy application. This can be more difficult than it appears (especially when it is done well), because policy applications are legitimately fraught with institutional features and exceptions to the simple frameworks used by academics. But the simple frameworks have the advantage of cutting through unnecessary detail to reveal the essential features of the issue. In my reading, the authors strike this balance carefully. While we can always quibble about what constitutes the essential features of an issue, the authors have a framework that highlights the issues they emphasize.

Figure 1-1 demonstrates the importance of the issues at hand. The figure shows that the maturity structure of Treasury debt lengthened over the last decade or so, as it often does when the debt-to-GDP ratio rises. The Treasury's traditional argument for lengthening the maturity structure is simple: the Treasury is generally interested in financing the nation's debt at the lowest cost and greatest stability. Long rates appeared relatively favorable over this period relative to historical levels, though not relative to short rates (more on this point later). Looking at the same data, the Federal Reserve had a different objective: It wanted to put downward pressure on the rates of longer-term non-Treasury assets to promote private investment and economic activity for entities that cannot borrow at the Treasury rate. Hence, the Fed purchased long-term Treasuries (and agency mortgage-backed securities) and held them on their balance sheet. So to the extent that the amount of Treasury debt in the hands of the public influenced the effectiveness of quantitative easing, the Treasury was working at cross-purposes to the Fed. The conclusion of this logic is that the Treasury can't have it both ways: it can't both minimize its cost of funding and support countercyclical debt management policy, at least in the circumstances of the financial crisis.

This episode is a natural place to begin a broader discussion of the objectives of Treasury debt management and the maturity structure of the Federal debt. This chapter identifies four broad objectives: (1) minimize funding cost, (2) stability of financing, (3) countercyclical aggregate demand policy, and (4) liquidity and financial stability. The first two are the traditional objectives identified by debt managers; the second two have been highlighted more recently in light of the financial crisis and unconventional monetary policies. This chapter investigates the quantitative importance of the cost factors in (1) and (2), and what we have learned so far about (3), which will be covered further in chapter 2, while drawing greater attention to the role of (4), which is the most difficult to quantify.

As soon as we identify multiple objectives for a single tool, in this case the maturity structure of the debt, we are likely to face trade-offs. The authors' first quantitative point is that these objectives need not always be at cross-purposes. When the Treasury term premium was higher, the authors argue that cost minimization would have argued for financing the national debt at shorter maturities. Their counterfactual calculations suggest that the savings from rolling over short-term debt would have been substantial. (The authors acknowledge that this is an ex post exercise, since we don't know what pricing and market dynamics would have been if the Treasury really had issued shorter and rolled over more frequently.) But the exercise suggests cost savings from a shorter tenure of debt and a more coherent debt management policy that both reduced costs and supported countercyclical monetary policy, along with providing more liquidity in the form of short-term Treasuries. In some ways this is the best quantitative argument: when all of these objectives point in the same direction, debt management should clearly follow. While this seems like a win-win-win for the Treasury, a broader view of cost minimization includes the authors' second objective of debt management, which is to avoid fiscal volatility or disruption. A financing strategy that minimizes short-term costs at the risk of funding volatility (or, in the extreme, a run or an auction failure) is not cost minimizing in a dynamic sense. The Treasury's focus on extending the maturity of the debt had this second, more dynamic, objective in mind. But this extension just puts the "you can't have it both ways" argument into a new perspective: the Treasury can't use maturity structure alone to promote fiscal stability and three other goals that lean toward a shorter maturity structure (at least for a time).

The lengthening of maturities during the financial crisis is not unusual; the authors document that the Treasury tends to lengthen the duration of debt when the national debt rises. In a country that does not have the "exorbitant privilege" associated with the world's reserve currency and safe assets, this may be a response to rollover risk and the desire to mitigate fiscal risk and the probability of a self-fulfilling run on the debt. In the recent U.S. experience, this possibility seems remote, though debt managers go to great lengths to ensure that debt issuance is predictable and reliable. This is in service of the objective to minimize the cost of funding the debt while taking into account the cost of longer-run fiscal risk.

The apparent cost advantage of short-term debt need not always be the case; the recent yield curve does not show such term premia and the benefits of shorter-term financing have eroded. In the current environment, financing longer term looks more favorable for cost minimization, and hence more at odds with the goals of countercyclical demand management and quantitative easing. Recent work on the bond-stock returns correlations suggests that these correlations have reversed in the last decade, eroding the term premium and making long-term Treasury issuance more attractive (see, for example, Song 2014). In this case, both aspects of cost minimization go in the direction of funding at longer maturities and counter to the objective of demand management as implemented through quantitative easing. Hence, the very strongest case for reducing the duration of Treasury debt seems to have been episodic and weaker now, though more conventional trade-offs are still present.

Cost minimization, in a dynamic sense, has traditionally been the primary focus of Treasury's debt management; this can lead to either a greater emphasis on issuing at short maturities or at longer maturities, depending upon the term premium. The liquidity premium is a distinct consideration. For cost minimization, this chapter's advice, as stated in the summary, is simple: "catering to liquidity premia and economizing on term premia." While it is difficult to quantify the value of liquidity in the economy, given the importance of liquidity during the financial crisis, this argument pushes toward funding shorter as a financial stability tool. However, if liquidity provision for financial stability is the issue, there are other tools at the government's disposal. For example, if liquidity premia are associated with "on the run" bonds, this chapter suggests issuing more of these (which can be longer maturity) and paying them off early.[25] Alternatively, there has been discussion of segregated reserve accounts, reverse repurchase agreements, and other measures to provide liquidity at scale. The Treasury need not distort its debt issuance as the only mechanism to meet all demand for liquidity. Of course, the presence of alternative (competing) liquid assets may affect the rate of return on liquid Treasuries, and in particular, Treasuries may not command such a premium if there are substantial alternative mechanisms for liquidity provision.

Finally, on implementation, it is worth noting that many agencies in the government have overlapping mandates and fragmented responsibilities, as do the Treasury and the Federal Reserve. Fragmented authority is common in government and in democracies in general to avoid concentration of power. But taking into account broader policy objectives even with limited authority is common practice. For example, the Department of Justice, the Federal Communications Commission (FCC), and the Federal Trade Commission (FTC) all work on antitrust policy, where the stakes are high and the public-private engagement is often contentious. The authority and mandate of each agency is limited, and they have carved up responsibility for various aspects of the merger approval process while still maintaining the same broad objectives of public good. That is, divided authority need not lead to divergent objectives and actions.

Quantitatively, the authors argue for using the consolidated government debt as the relevant metric for debt management: accumulated Treasury

---

25. Though, if this strategy was known, pricing would surely change to reflect the true expected duration of the bonds.

issuance less what is held by the Fed. For many of the questions asked in the chapter, this is the appropriate measure, but not for all questions. For the aggregate demand management issues emphasized and the impact of QE, subtracting out Fed holdings is entirely appropriate. For other objectives of debt management, netting out Fed holdings sacrifices information. To evaluate cost minimization, for example, the Treasury would want to know if bonds are on "special" (such as being on the run) and whether they are held domestically or abroad (for Ricardian reasons), not only what is held outside the Fed. Similarly, while rollover risk seems remote, conceptually, the Treasury bears the risk of rapidly escalating costs if such an event were to occur. Even if all of the maturing Treasuries were held by the government (so on a consolidated basis there appears to be little short-term debt outstanding), rolling over securities into new auctions would be the responsibility of the Treasury. For example, the current Fed holdings need not roll over into new Fed holdings unless there is a dynamic and credible commitment to do so. Finally, even if Treasuries are held by the Fed, they could potentially be made available for private liquidity through the repo market, so netting them out would understate available Treasury liquidity. Hence, a consolidated approach nets out information that is valuable to address some of the four objectives identified for debt management.

The trade-offs involved among these four objectives are difficult to weight and quantify. This chapter makes a serious effort to establish the relative importance of factors favoring short-term versus longer-term financing. Their advice is really a nudge—that the argument for lengthening maturity is generally weaker than we thought and the argument for shortening is stronger. Even if one is convinced by the argument that the Treasury should have taken into account the arguments for quantitative easing and considered less extension of the maturity structure, how much less? Or did the Treasury already take into account Fed purchases given its objective of cost minimization? Greenwood, Hanson, Rudolph, and Summers provide some quantitative measures of term premia and fiscal risk, leading them to put a "thumb on the scale" for more short-term debt issuance to provide more short-term liquid assets and less longer-term debt to the market. Those involved in debt management would emphasize cost minimization dynamically and argue for locking in low rates. However remote rollover risk appears given the "exorbitant privilege" afforded the dollar and U.S. Treasuries, experience also suggests that the dynamics around a panic or a run can be highly nonlinear. In a financial crisis and thereafter, there is a strong argument for issuing short-term securities for liquidity provision and financial stability, a relatively new consideration in maturity management. Alternative measures involving regulation and supervision do not "get in all the cracks" (Stein 2013) the way that Treasuries do, suggesting a unique role for near-money Treasury assets. But quantifying how much Treasury supply is needed and at what maturities to fill that role remains an open question. These are all quantitative policy choices, yet we still lack a complete framework in which to balance them.

These qualms about quantitative recommendations should be taken as a call for analysis, not as a recommendation for paralysis. This chapter provides a framework and four main objectives for debt management, adding in two—aggregate demand and financial stability—not on the traditional list. The inclusion of these concerns follows directly from experience during the financial crisis. Even if we don't yet have a detailed roadmap for policy, this is the right discussion at the right time.

COMMENT

Brian Sack

The Treasury has managed its debt in an effective manner, allowing it to fund a sizable debt stock at relatively low interest rates. Investors place considerable value on the safety and liquidity of Treasury securities, giving the Treasury's extensive borrowing capacity at all times, even during periods of market stress. These characteristics of Treasury debt reflect many factors, but sound debt management decisions have certainly contributed to them.

These comments are based in part on the presentation I made at the 2014 Roundtable on Treasury Markets and Debt Management held by the Treasury on December 5, 2014. I thank Derek Kaufman for his feedback on these comments and Evan Wu for his assistance in preparing them. All views expressed here, and any errors, are my own and do not represent in any way the views of The D. E. Shaw Group.

This success has come despite the absence of a clear analytical framework for understanding the debt management decisions made by Treasury. Treasury officials have at times made general comments about the goals of debt management, noting the Treasury's focus on achieving the lowest cost of funding. However, these comments have not fully identified all aspects of the objective function of debt management.

As a result, while debt management decisions have been made in directions that seem intuitive, it is difficult to rigorously assess them or to calibrate how far they should go. Consider, for example, the current discussion of the weighted average maturity of outstanding Treasury debt. The average maturity has risen markedly from its trough in 2008 and is set to move well above its historical range under current issuance patterns—an outcome that some might argue is desirable in the current environment of a low-term premium. However, without a more complete description of the Treasury's objectives, it is difficult to assess how far this pattern should extend, or even to determine all of the issues that should affect this decision.

For these reasons, it is an important exercise to more rigorously define the objective function of U.S. debt management. In this regard, the chapter by Greenwood, Hanson, Rudolph, and Summers makes a valuable contribution. The authors present a thorough discussion of the most relevant debt management issues and push beyond the standard perspective by raising some additional considerations.

The authors say that there should be four objectives for debt management: "(1) financing the government at least cost by catering to liquidity premia and economizing on term premia; (2) limiting fiscal risk, particularly that associated with short-term financing; (3) managing aggregate demand by using the maturity of government debt to influence long-term interest rates; and (4) promoting financial stability by issuing enough short-term government debt to counteract the financial system's tendency toward excessive liquidity transformation."

I will begin with the first two items, because they are the key considerations in most discussions of debt management. As the authors discuss, these two items present a trade-off when considering the maturity of the debt being issued. Issuing longer-term debt generally involves paying a higher expected funding cost, at least when the term premium is positive (meaning that long-term rates are higher than the expected path of short-term rates to compensate investors for duration risk). In return, by locking in its funding cost for a longer time, the Treasury reduces the amount of fiscal risk, the extent to which changes in interest expenses could require costly adjustments to government expenditures and taxation rates.

The authors' discussion of these two considerations does an effective job of bridging the theoretical results from the economics literature with the practical issues that debt managers face. My reactions focus on some challenges involved with applying this framework:

The term premium, though well defined in theory, is difficult to measure: We have many different models of the term premium, each providing a different measure. Two of the best-known models, by Kim and Wright (2005) and Adrian, Crump, and Moench (2013), come from the staff of the Federal Reserve. Nevertheless, the resulting measures for the ten-year term premium have differed by more than 150 basis points (bps) at times, with an average absolute gap of 83 bps over the past ten years. In practice, debt managers would have to settle on which measures to use and be cognizant of the uncertainty around them. An additional complication is that the authors argue that it is only the component of the term premium associated with liquidity services that should be considered—a potentially important consideration that makes its measurement even more challenging.

The expected path of the term premium matters: Because debt management decisions today inevitably will have consequences for the patterns of issuance that will be needed in the future, debt management decisions need to be forward looking. In particular, it is not just the term premium today that matters in decisions, but also its expected evolution going forward. Various empirical studies of the term premium have found components that should have some degree of predictability—for example, Cochrane and Piazzesi (2005) argue that there is a countercyclical factor. A full debt management framework would have to take these dynamics into account.

The correlation of interest rates and funding needs may vary over time: The authors point out that it is not the variation in interest costs that matters, but the consequences of that variation for the overall fiscal position. This is important: if short-term interest rates are negatively correlated with the structural budget deficit, issuing short-term debt could actually provide the government with a hedge that makes it easier to run countercyclical fiscal policy. This correlation, however, could vary over time depending on the types of shocks that are hitting the economy. The negative correlation mentioned previously might be expected if the economy is being hit by shocks to aggregate demand, but shocks to inflation or changes in inflation expectations could generate the opposite pattern.

Debt managers' objective function is more complicated: I appreciate the fact that the authors presented a specific objective function, and therefore could derive a first-order condition for maximizing that objective function. However, the objective function they consider is obviously oversimplified— it involves a one-time decision on the optimal fraction between two types of debt. It will be important to reach a more general specification that allows for different maturity points, appropriately calibrates the fiscal risk component, and considers the full trajectory of the debt profile when making decisions today.

The social benefits of issuing across the yield curve are important: One aspect of the objective function that the authors mention as an "additional consideration" is the nonpecuniary value of issuing at maturity points across the yield curve. Doing so provides benchmarks for risk-free interest rates at various maturities and may facilitate hedging and pricing in other markets. In my view, this objective should be elevated to be a primary consideration in the objective function. It may be hard to calibrate the social benefits, but having these risk-free debt securities seems to be an important aspect of the functioning of fixed-income markets.

So where does this leave us? I argue for a three-part objective function that takes into account the expected cost of the debt, the amount of fiscal risk, and the benefit from issuing across the curve. In addition, the framework should likely include adjustment costs that slow the adjustment of issuance patterns in response to this objective function, in order to reduce near-term uncertainty in the market. This last term would correspond to Treasury's preference for "regular and predictable" issuance.

In contrast, I feel that the case for the third and fourth objectives mentioned in this chapter is less compelling, or at least involves more unanswered questions.

I simply disagree that the third objective—managing aggregate demand— should be part of the objective function of debt management. It is not clear to me why Treasury debt issuance should seek to have an expansionary impact on the economy, as the authors advocate, when the Federal Reserve is already operating with a mandate for the economy. The Fed is charged with setting financial conditions in the manner necessary to achieve maximum employment and low inflation. Efforts by the Treasury to use a separate policy instrument to achieve one part of the Fed's mandate would likely be counterproductive under normal market circumstances; the mandates would not always be aligned, and the presence of two active policy institutions would create confusion and communication challenges. Instead, the Treasury should make its debt management decisions focused on its other objectives, and the Fed should simply take into account any economic effects of those decisions when deciding on the appropriate stance of monetary policy.

On the fourth objective—promoting financial stability—it is worth having this discussion, but in my view there remain some unresolved issues. The authors focus on one particular source of financial instability—the tendency of private markets to create excessive amounts of money-like instruments—and argue that greater Treasury bill issuance could crowd out some of that activity. I am sympathetic to that argument, as I think the financial system would function better with a greater supply of short-term risk-free instruments. However, introducing a financial stability objective into debt management raises some challenging questions.

I worry about the scope of such a mandate—if other perceived vulnerabilities emerge that could be influenced by maturity supply, would Treasury then be obligated to respond with debt management decisions? I worry about the implementation of such a mandate—is Treasury supposed to monitor private sector maturity transformation and adjust the supply of bills in a discretionary manner in response? And I worry that debt management is not really the appropriate tool for addressing financial stability concerns—isn't financial regulation intended for these purposes? In short, it might simply be too great of a burden for debt management to take on financial stability issues.

Overall, this chapter advances our understanding of the framework that should govern debt management decisions. I hope it leads to further refinement of the parts of the objective function that clearly belong, and additional discussion of the parts that are more debatable. In the end, we should hope to arrive at a more explicit and comprehensive description of the goals of debt management and hence better grasp the optimal structure of the public debt.

References

Adrian, Tobias, Richard K. Crump, and Emanuel Moench. 2013. "Pricing the Term Structure with Linear Regressions." *Journal of Financial Economics* 110, no. 1 (October): 110–38.

Amihud, Yakov, and Haim Mendelson. 1991. "Asset Prices and Financial Policy." *Financial Analysts Journal* 47, no. 6 (November): 56–66.

Auerbach, Alan J., and William G. Gale. 2009. "The Economic Crisis and the Fiscal Crisis, 2009 and Beyond." *Tax Notes* 125, no. 1 (October): 101–30.

Barro, Robert J. 1974. "Are Government Bonds Net Wealth?" *Journal of Political Economy* 82, no. 6 (November–December): 1095–117.

———. 1979. "On the Determination of the Public Debt." *Journal of Political Economy* 87, no. 5 (October): 940–71.

Bernanke, Ben, Vincent R. Reinhart, and Brian P. Sack. 2004. "Monetary Policy Alternatives at the Zero Bound: An Empirical Assessment." *Brookings Papers on Economic Activity* no. 2: 1–100.

Campbell, John Y., Robert J. Shiller, and Luis M. Viceira. 2009. "Understanding Inflation-Indexed Bond Markets." *Brookings Papers on Economic Activity* (Spring): 79–120.

Carlson, Mark, Burcu Duygan-Bump, Fabio Natalucci, William R. Nelson, Marcelo Ochoa, Jeremy Stein, and Skander Van den Heuvel. 2014. "The Demand for Short-Term, Safe Assets and Financial Stability: Some Evidence and Implications for Central Bank Policies," FEDS Working Paper 2014-102 (Washington, D.C.: Federal Reserve Board of Governors).

Chetty, Raj. 2012. "Bounds on Elasticities with Optimization Frictions: A Synthesis of Micro and Macro Evidence on Labor Supply." *Econometrica* 80: 969–1018.

Cochrane, John H. 2001. "Long-Term Debt and Optimal Policy in the Fiscal Theory of the Price Level." *Econometrica* 69, no. 1 (January): 69–116.

———. 2014. "Monetary Policy with Interest on Reserves," mimeo, September.

Cochrane, John H., and Monika Piazzesi. 2005. "Bond Risk Premia." *American Economic Review* 95, no. 1 (March): 138–60.

Duffee, Gregory R. 1996. "Idiosyncratic Variation of Treasury Bill Yields." *Journal of Financial Studies* 24: 2895–934.

Ferguson, Niall, Andreas Schaab, and Moritz Schularick. 2014. "Central Bank Balance Sheets: Expansion and Reduction since 1900," ECB Forum on Central Banking.

Fleckenstein, Matthias, Francis A. Longstaff, and Hanno Lustig. 2014. "The TIPS–Treasury Bond Puzzle." *Journal of Finance* 69: 2151–2197.

Fleming, Michael J. 2000. "The Benchmark U.S. Treasury Market: Recent Performance and Possible Alternatives." Federal Reserve Bank of New York, *Economic Policy Review* 6, no. 1 (April): 129–45.

Friedman, Milton. 1960. *A Program for Monetary Stability*. Fordham University Press.

Gagnon, Joseph, Matthew Raskin, Julie Remache, and Brian Sack. 2011. "Large-Scale Asset Purchases by the Federal Reserve: Did They Work?" Federal Reserve Bank of New York Staff Report 441, March.

Garbade, Kenneth, and Matthew Rutherford. 2007. "Buybacks in Treasury Cash and Debt Management." Federal Reserve Bank of New York Staff Report 304.

Gensler, Gary. 1998. Remarks before the President's Commission to Study Capital Budgeting (www.treasury.gov/press-center/press-releases/Pages/rr2493.aspx).

Gorton, Gary B. 2010. *Slapped by the Invisible Hand: The Panic of 2007.* Oxford University Press.

Gorton, Gary B., and Andrew Metrick. 2012. "Who Ran on Repo?" NBER Working Paper 18455 (Cambridge, Mass.: National Bureau of Economic Research).

Greenwood, Robin, Samuel G. Hanson, and Jeremy C. Stein. 2010. "A Gap-Filling Theory of Corporate Debt Maturity Choice." *Journal of Finance* 65, no. 3: 993–1028.

———. 2015. "A Comparative Advantage Approach to Government Debt Maturity." *Journal of Finance* 70: 1683–722.

Greenwood, Robin, and Dimitri Vayanos. 2010. "Price Pressure in the Government Bond Market." *American Economic Review* 100, no. 2: 585–90.

———. 2014. "Bond Supply and Excess Bond Returns." *Review of Financial Studies* 27, no. 3: 663–713.

Gurkaynak, Refet S., Brian Sack, and Jonathan H. Wright. 2007. "The U.S. Treasury Yield Curve: 1961 to the Present." *Journal of Monetary Economics* 54, no. 8: 2291–304.

———. 2010. "The TIPS Yield Curve and Inflation Compensation." *American Economic Journal: Macroeconomics* 2, no. 1: 70–92.

Hanson, Samuel G. 2014. "Mortgage Convexity." *Journal of Financial Economics* 113, no. 2 (August): 270–99.

Jarrow, Robert A., and Hao Li. 2012. "The Impact of Quantitative Easing on the U.S. Term Structure of Interest Rates," Johnson School Research Paper 2-2012.

Kashyap, Anil K., and Jeremy C. Stein. 2012. "The Optimal Conduct of Monetary Policy with Interest on Reserves." *American Economic Journal: Macroeconomics* 4, no. 1 (January): 266–82.

Kim, Don H., and Jonathan H. Wright. 2005. "An Arbitrage-Free Three-Factor Term Structure Model and the Recent Behavior of Long-Term Yields and Distant-Horizon Forward Rates," Finance and Economics Discussion Series 2005-33 (Board of Governors of the Federal Reserve System).

Krishnamurthy, Arvind. 2002. "The Bond/Old-Bond Spread." *Journal of Financial Economics* 66, no. 2 (November): 463–506.

Krishnamurthy, Arvind, and Annette Vissing-Jorgensen. 2011. "The Effects of Quantitative Easing on Interest Rates: Channels and Implications for Policy." *Brookings Papers on Economic Activity* (Fall): 215–65.

———. 2012. "The Aggregate Demand for Treasury Debt." *Journal of Political Economy* 120, no. 2 (April): 233–67.

———. 2013. "The Ins and Outs of Large Scale Asset Purchases," Kansas City Federal Reserve Symposium on Global Dimensions of Unconventional Monetary Policy (www.kansascityfed.org/publicat/sympos/2013/2013Krishnamurthy.pdf).

Leeper, Eric M. 1991. "Equilibria under 'Active' and 'Passive' Monetary and Fiscal Policies." *Journal of Monetary Economics* 27, no. 1 (February): 129–47.

Li, Canlin, and Min Wei. 2013. "Term Structure Modeling with Supply Factors and the Federal Reserve's Large-Scale Asset Purchase Programs." *International Journal of Central Banking* 9, no. 1: 3–39.

Lucas, Robert, Jr., and Nancy L. Stokey. 1983. "Optimal Fiscal and Monetary Policy in an Economy without Capital." *Journal of Monetary Economics* 12, no. 1: 55–93.

Malkhozov, Aytek, Phillippe Mueller, Andrea Vedolin, and Gyuri Venter. 2014. "Funding Liquidity CAPM: International Evidence," unpublished working paper.

Modigliani, Franco, and Merton Miller. 1958. "The Cost of Capital, Corporation Finance and the Theory of Investment." *American Economic Review* 48, no. 3: 261–297.

Nagel, Stefan. 2014. "The Liquidity Premium of Near-Money Assets," NBER Working Paper 20265 (Cambridge, Mass.: National Bureau of Economic Research).

Pflueger, Carolin E., and Luis M. Viceira. 2013. "Return Predictability in the Treasury Market: Real Rates, Inflation, and Liquidity," working paper (Cambridge, Mass.: Harvard University Business School).

Piketty, Thomas. 2014. *Capital in the Twenty-First Century*. Harvard University Press.

Poterba, James M., and Lawrence H. Summers. 1987. "Finite Lifetimes and the Effects of Budget Deficits on National Saving." *Journal of Monetary Economics* 20, no. 2 (September): 369–91.

Pozsar, Zoltan. 2011. "Institutional Cash Pools and the Triffin Dilemma of the U.S. Banking System," IMF Working Paper 11/190 (Washington, D.C.: International Monetary Fund).

———. 2012. "A Macro View of Shadow Banking: Do T-Bill Shortages Pose a New Triffin Dilemma?" in *Is U.S. Government Debt Different?* edited by Franklin Allen and others (Philadelphia: FIC Press), pp. 35–44.

Ramanathan, Karthik. 2008. "Overview of U.S. Debt Management" (www.treasury.gov/about/organizational-structure/offices/Domestic-Finance/Documents/Treas_DebtMgmt_Overview.ppt).

Reinhart, Carmen, and M. Belen Sbrancia. 2011. "The Liquidation of Government Debts," NBER Working Paper 16893 (Cambridge, Mass.: National Bureau of Economic Research).

Ricks, Morgan. 2013. "A Simpler Approach to Financial Reform," SSRN Scholarly Paper (Rochester, N.Y.: Social Science Research Network), August.

Rudolph, Joshua. 2014. "The Interaction between Government Debt Management and Monetary Policy: A Call to Develop a Debt Maturity Framework for the Zero Lower Bound," master's thesis, Kennedy School of Government, Harvard University.

Sachs, Lee. 1999. "Statement before the House Committee on Ways and Means. Hearing on Treasury's Debt Buyback Proposal," September.

Sims, Christopher A. 1994. "A Simple Model for Study of the Determination of the Price Level and the Interaction of Monetary and Fiscal Policy." *Economic Theory* 4, no. 3: 381–99.

Song, Donho. 2014. "Bond Market Exposures to Macroeconomic and Monetary Policy Risks," unpublished working paper, November.

Stein, Jeremy C. 2012. "Monetary Policy as Financial-Stability Regulation." *Quarterly Journal of Economics* 127: 57–95.

———. 2013. "Overheating in Credit Markets: Origins, Measurement, and Policy Responses," Federal Reserve Bank of St. Louis, February (www.federalreserve.gov/newsevents/speech/stein20130207a.htm).

Summers, Lawrence H. 1997. "Inflation Indexed Securities in Treasury's Borrowing Program" (www.treasury.gov/press-center/press-releases/Pages/rr1966.aspx).

Sunderam, Adi. 2014. "Money Creation and the Shadow Banking System," mimeo, August.

Swanson, Eric. 2011. "Let's Twist Again: A High-Frequency Event Study Analysis of Operation Twist and Its Implications for QE2." *Brookings Papers on Economic Activity* (Spring): 151–207.

Tobin, James. 1958. "Liquidity Preference as Behavior towards Risk." *Review of Economic Studies* 25, no. 1: 65–86.

Treasury Borrowing Advisory Committee. 2009. Report to the Secretary of the Treasury, November (www.treasury.gov/press-center/press-releases/Pages/tg348.aspx).

Vayanos, Dimitri, and Jean-Luc Vila. 2009. "A Preferred-Habitat Model of the Term Structure of Interest Rates," Discussion Paper 641 (Financial Markets Group, London School of Economics and Political Science).

Vayanos, Dimitri, and Pierre-Oliver Weill. 2008. "A Search-Based Theory of the On-the-Run Phenomenon." *Journal of Finance* 63, no. 3 (June): 1361–98.

Warga, Arthur. 1992. "Bond Returns, Liquidity, and Missing Data." *Journal of Financial and Quantitative Analysis* 27, no. 4 (December): 605–17.

Wessel, David. 1993. "Bond Market Gives Boost to Officials Seeking to Alter Treasury Financing Mix." *Wall Street Journal*, January 25.

Woodford, Michael. 1995. "Price-Level Determinacy without Control of a Monetary Aggregate." *Carnegie-Rochester Conference Series on Public Policy* 43, no. 1 (December): 1–46.

———. 2012. "Methods of Policy Accommodation at the Interest-Rate Lower Bound." Paper presented at the Jackson Hole symposium, August.

2

DEBT MANAGEMENT CONFLICTS BETWEEN THE U.S. TREASURY AND THE FEDERAL RESERVE

Robin Greenwood, Samuel G. Hanson,
Joshua S. Rudolph, and Lawrence H. Summers

In this chapter, we discuss conflicts between the U.S. Treasury and the Federal Reserve in their debt management operations. Our use of the term "debt management operations" is not a conventional way to describe Federal Reserve policy, but we use it here to recognize the role that the Fed has in influencing the net supply of debt held by the public.

We start by documenting empirically the extent to which monetary and fiscal policies have been pushing in opposite directions in recent years. We show that, despite successive rounds of quantitative easing (QE), the stock of government debt with a maturity over five years that is held by the public (excluding the Fed's holdings) has risen from 8 percent of GDP at the end of 2007 to 15 percent at the middle of 2014. Pressure on bond investors to absorb long-term government debt has actually increased rather than decreased over the last six years!

We find that between two-thirds and three-quarters of the increased supply of longer-term Treasuries is explained by the dramatic growth in outstanding debt due to the large deficits associated with the Great Recession.

The remaining one-quarter to one-third is due to the Treasury's active policy of extending the average maturity of its debt.

In discussions of its QE policies, the Federal Reserve has focused on the effects that its bond purchases were expected to have on long-term interest rates and, by extension, the economy more broadly. However, in doing so, it completely ignored any possible impact on government fiscal risk, even though the Federal Reserve's profits and losses are remitted to the Treasury. Treasury's debt management announcements and the advice of the Treasury Borrowing Advisory Committee (TBAC), a committee of investment managers and bankers who meet regularly to advise the Treasury debt managers, have focused on the assumed benefits of extending the average debt maturity from a fiscal risk perspective and largely ignored the impact of policy changes on long-term yields. To the extent that the Federal Reserve and Treasury ever publicly mention the other's mandate, it is usually in the context of avoiding the perception that one institution might be helping the other achieve an objective. The Fed does not want to be seen as monetizing deficits. The Treasury has been reluctant to acknowledge the role that the Fed has in debt management—the Treasury effectively treats the Fed as nothing more than a large investor.

We then place the current tension between Federal Reserve–led debt management and Treasury-led debt management in historical perspective. Before 2008, changes in Federal Reserve holdings of long-term bonds had only a tiny impact on the amount of long-term Treasury debt held by the public—that is, Fed policy had little direct impact on the consolidated debt management strategy of the U.S. government. However, we describe a few historical examples in which the Federal Reserve and the Treasury agreed to coordinate policy for the purpose of achieving a common set of objectives with regard to debt management. Thus, history suggests that greater cooperation on debt management is possible.

We argue that improved cooperation between the Treasury and the Federal Reserve in setting debt management policy would be in the national interest. We outline the principles that would form the basis for such cooperation. In sketching this framework, we draw on the arguments we developed in chapter 1, where we laid out a trade-off model for the management of the *consolidated* government debt. According to this model, optimal debt maturity trades off objectives of financing the government at the lowest cost and at a suitable level of refinancing risk (typically considerations taken up by the Treasury) with considerations related to financial stability and aggregate demand management (typically considerations taken up by the central bank). Given these objectives, it is straightforward to describe settings in which, under current institutional arrangements, the Treasury may come into conflict with the Federal Reserve because it places different weights on the competing objectives of debt management. While the potential for conflict is greatest when interest rates are at the zero lower bound, we suggest that a lack of coordination can lead to suboptimal policy during ordinary times as well, although the costs are not as great then because the Fed can offset debt management decisions by moving the short-term interest rate.

During normal times conflict can arise because there are only two policy instruments—the short-term interest rate and debt management—but at least four policy objectives. Improved policy coordination could reduce these conflicts, especially when the conflicts are exacerbated when interest rates are very low. At the zero lower bound, a fully coordinated policy—such as the policy the Treasury and the Fed already pursue with respect to currency intervention—should be the norm.

Fed versus Treasury: 2008–14

Starting in 2008, U.S. monetary policy and debt management dramatically changed course in response to the unfolding financial and economic crisis, pulling the government balance sheet in opposite directions.

Table 2-1 shows a stylized depiction of the major financial assets and liabilities of the U.S. government in December 2007 and July 2014. The size of the Federal Reserve's balance sheet has grown fivefold over this period due to its purchases of $1.8 trillion of long-term Treasuries and $1.8 trillion of mortgage-backed securities (MBS) and agency securities, financed by an increase in interest-bearing reserves.[1] The duration of the Federal Reserve's

---

1. The initial surge in the Fed's balance sheet occurred after Lehman Brothers' failure in September 2008 and was due to lending to private intermediaries and firms under various liquidity facilities. Since early 2009, the Fed balance sheet growth has been due to large-scale asset purchases (LSAPs), often referred to as quantitative easing (QE).

Historically, the Fed did not pay interest on reserves and instead controlled short-term nominal interest rates by varying the supply of reserves to target a desired level for the rate on overnight loans between banks (the Federal funds rate). However, central banks in many other countries control short-term rates by paying

Table 2-1. *Consolidated U.S. Government Balance Sheet: 2007 versus 2014*

Assets	December 2007		July 2014		Liabilities	December 2007		July 2014	
	FV ($tr)	Dur (yrs)	FV ($tr)	Dur (yrs)		FV ($tr)	Dur (yrs)	FV ($tr)	Dur (yrs)
Federal Reserve									
Treasury Debt	$0.7	3.3	$2.5	7.8	Currency	$0.8	N/A	$1.2	N/A
MBS + Agency Debt	$0.0	N/A	$1.8	5.6	Reserves	$0.01	0.0	$2.7	0.0
Other	$0.1	N/A	$0.1	N/A	Other	$0.1	0.0	$0.4	0.0
Treasury									
Taxing Power	N/A	N/A	N/A	N/A	Treasury debt	$4.5	3.9	$12.2	4.6
Consolidated balance sheet									
					Treasury debt	$3.8	4.1	$9.6	3.8
Taxing Power	N/A	N/A	N/A	N/A	Currency	$0.8	N/A	$1.2	N/A
MBS + Agency Debt	$0.0	N/A	$1.8	5.6	Reserves	$0.01	0.0	$2.7	0.0
Other	$0.1	N/A	$0.1	N/A	Other	$0.1	0.0	$0.4	0.0
Total	**$0.1**	**N/A**	**$1.9**	**N/A**	**Total**	**$4.6**	**4.0**	**$14.0**	**2.9**

Sources: Based on authors' calculations using data from the Treasury's Monthly Statement of the Public Debt, the Federal Reserve System's H.4.1 Release (Factors Affecting Reserve Balances), and the Federal Reserve Bank of New York's System Open Market Account Holdings release.

Note: FV denotes face value of the claim in trillions of U.S. dollars, and *Dur* denotes the Macaulay duration in years, as estimated by the authors based on the July 2014 yield curve. Consolidation nets out the Treasury debt that is held by the Federal Reserve.

portfolio of Treasury securities increased from 3.3 years to 7.8 years.[2] At the same time, Treasury debt outstanding rose from 31 percent of GDP in 2007 to 70 percent of GDP in 2014. The duration of the outstanding Treasury debt increased from 3.9 years to 4.6 years. On a consolidated basis, however, the duration of the U.S. government's liabilities has moved very little, from 4.0 years to 2.9 years, as table 2-1 shows.

interest on reserves. The Fed obtained the authority to pay interest on reserves under the Emergency Economic Stabilization Act of 2008.

2. Duration is the weighted average time to receipt of the cash flows on a bond. Duration captures the sensitivity of a bond's price to its yield and is an indicator of how much interest rate risk is being borne by a bondholder.

We isolate the policy-driven component of these changes and assess the net impact of these policies by converting them into common and economically meaningful units of interest rate risk. We start with the Federal Reserve's balance sheet, summarized in panel A of table 2-2 at year-end dates beginning in December 2007. The vast majority of the securities held by the Federal Reserve System are held in the System Open Market Account (SOMA). In December 2007, securities held in the SOMA had a face value of $750 billion. These securities were comprised of mostly Treasury bills, notes, and bonds, with an average duration of 3.3 years, similar to the duration of outstanding Treasury debt. After falling in 2008, by December 2009 the face value of all securities in the SOMA had reached $1,839 billion, including $771 billion of Treasury securities, $160 billion of debt issued by Fannie Mae and Freddie Mac, and $908 billion of MBS guaranteed by Fannie Mae and Freddie Mac and the Government National Mortgage Association (GNMA). By July 2014, the securities held by the SOMA had doubled again, reaching $4,121 billion (58 percent in U.S. Treasuries, 41 percent in MBS, 1 percent Fannie Mae and Freddie Mac debt). Thus, the total increase from 2007 was $3,371 billion, or 19.4 percent of 2014 GDP.

To estimate the impact of QE—as opposed to the normal growth in the size of the Fed's balance sheet due to the growth in the demand for currency in circulation—we adjust the growth in the SOMA for growth during ordinary times. A simple way to do this is based on the observation that from 2003 to 2007 the SOMA averaged 95 percent of currency in circulation. Thus, we estimate the abnormal growth in the Fed's balance sheet due to QE by subtracting 0.95 times currency in circulation. The third column in panel A of table 2-2 shows that this adjustment implies a cumulative *abnormal* growth in the Fed's balance sheet of $2.9 trillion between December 2007 and July 2014.

If one's objective is simply to assess the scale of the Federal Reserve's balance sheet, one could simply track the *face value* of its security holdings, as we have just done. However, the goal of QE was to reduce the amount of interest rate risk borne by private investors, thereby lowering long-term interest rates through a portfolio balance channel. Thus, the analysis is more informative if holdings are converted into common units. We do so by adjusting Federal Reserve holdings by their Macaulay duration, which captures the weighted average maturity of the debt.[3]

---

3. Vayanos and Vila (2009) and Greenwood and Vayanos (2014) show that bond supply shocks may impact term premia if they change the amount of interest rate risk that must be borne by fixed-income investors.

Table 2-2. *Quantitative Easing and Treasury Maturity Extension: Ten-Year Duration Equivalents*

| | Panel A: Impact of quantitative easing | | | | | | | Panel B: Impact of expansion of debt and Treasury maturity extension | | | | | | |
| | Fed holdings | | | | 10-year equivalents | | | Debt outstanding | | 10-year equivalents | | | |
	SOMA ($bn)	Currency ×0.95	QE ($bn)	Dur (yrs)	SOMA ($bn)	QE ($bn)	QE (% GDP)	Debt ($bn)	Dur (yrs)	Total ($bn)	Cum Δ (% GDP)	Debt expand (% GDP)	Mat extend (% GDP)
12/2007	750	784	0	3.3	279	0	0.0%	4,537	3.9	2,005	0.0%	0.0%	0.0%
12/2008	490	844	0	5.4	299	0	0.0%	5,798	3.5	2,287	1.9%	3.8%	-1.9%
12/2009	1,839	883	956	5.4	1,119	744	5.4%	7,272	3.9	3,189	8.1%	8.3%	-0.2%
12/2010	2,150	934	1,215	5.3	1,288	941	6.2%	8,863	4.1	4,101	13.8%	12.6%	1.2%
12/2011	2,604	1,020	1,584	5.6	1,655	1,276	8.1%	9,937	4.3	4,817	17.7%	15.1%	2.7%
12/2012	2,649	1,105	1,544	7.2	2,144	1,733	10.6%	11,053	4.5	5,535	21.5%	17.6%	4.0%
12/2013	3,743	1,178	2,564	7.0	2,938	2,500	14.6%	11,869	4.5	6,066	23.8%	19.0%	4.8%
7/2014	4,121	1,220	2,901	6.8	3,172	2,718	15.6%	12,163	4.6	6,339	24.9%	19.4%	5.5%

Source: Authors' calculations using data from the Federal Reserve System's H.4.1 Release (Factors Affecting Reserve Balances) and the Treasury's Monthly Statement of the Public Debt. GDP is from the Bureau of Economic Analysis.

Note: Panel A describes the impact of QE programs on the Federal Reserve balance sheet, at year-end dates beginning in December 2007. SOMA refers to the System Open Market Account. Between 2003 and 2007, the SOMA was an average of 95 percent of currency in circulation. We define QE impact to be SOMA minus 0.95× currency in circulation. To convert into ten-year duration equivalents, we multiply face values by the ratio of portfolio duration (denoted by *Dur*) to the duration of a ten-year bond (8.9 years). Duration is computed based on the July 2014 yield curve. Panel B describes the impact of U.S. Treasury's expansion and maturity extension of the public debt. We convert Treasuries outstanding into ten-year equivalents. We further break down the cumulative change in ten-year duration equivalents between December 2007 and July 2014 (estimated) into two components: the expansion of the debt and the maturity extension according to:

$$\Delta\left(\frac{\text{Debt}_t \cdot Dur_t}{Dur_t^{10\text{-}yr}}\right) = \left(\frac{1}{Dur_t^{10\text{-}yr}}\right) \cdot \left(\underbrace{\Delta\text{Debt}_t Dur_{t-1}}_{\text{Debt Expansion}} + \underbrace{\Delta Dur_t \text{Debt}_t}_{\text{Maturity Extension}}\right)$$

Duration of Federal Reserve Holdings and outstanding Treasury debt are computed by the authors as described in the text.

Specifically, we convert the Federal Reserve holdings into "ten-year duration equivalents" by multiplying the face value of the portfolio by its weighted average duration and dividing the result by the duration of a ten-year Treasury note.

$$\text{Debt}_t^{\text{10-yrEquivalent}} = \frac{\text{Debt}_t \cdot Dur_t}{Dur_t^{\text{10-yr}}}. \tag{2-1}$$

This calculation recognizes that, from the perspective of private investors, the amount of interest rate risk they are asked to bear would be the same if there were \$1 trillion twenty-year zero-coupon bonds as if there were \$2 trillion ten-year zero-coupon bonds.[4] Likewise, this calculation treats the purchase of \$1 billion ten-year zero-coupon Treasury bonds as equivalent to \$1 billion MBS with a duration of ten years. Put differently, this calculation implicitly assumes that the relevant policy instrument in the case of QE is the total amount of duration removed from the bond market.[5] Our conclusions here are not sensitive to methodology; we obtain similar results if we instead convert SOMA holdings and Treasury issuance into common units by simply rescaling by maturity.

To compute the duration of all securities in the SOMA, we combine our estimate of the average duration of the Fed's Treasury holdings with an estimate of the duration of its MBS and agency holdings. To isolate changes in duration due to changes in the Fed's holdings—as opposed to changes in the term structure of interest rates—we compute duration based on a constant yield curve on July 31, 2014. Table 2-2 shows that the combined duration impact of the Fed's QE policies, which is \$2,901 billion in face value

4. This is only strictly true if the yield curve shifts in a parallel fashion.
5. This is a clear simplification because it implies that it does not matter in which market the duration is purchased. In perfectly integrated fixed-income markets, a \$1 purchase of five-year duration MBS has the same policy impact as a \$1 purchase of five-year duration Treasuries. Krishnamurthy and Vissing-Jorgensen (2011, 2012) find strong evidence that the market for Treasury securities is partially segmented from agencies and MBS. At the same time, Hanson (2014) finds evidence that duration supply shocks in the MBS market are transmitted nearly one-for-one to the broader fixed-income market. Greenwood, Hanson, and Liao (2014) formally explore bond pricing dynamics in a setting in which a pair of markets is partially segmented in the short run, but is more integrated in the long run.

terms, was \$2,718 billion in ten-year equivalents, or 15.6 percent of GDP through July 2014.

In panel B of table 2-2, we describe the growth in outstanding Treasury debt since 2007 and the Treasury's decision to extend the maturity of the debt. We focus on marketable Treasury securities held by the public and the Federal Reserve. Data were obtained from the Monthly Statement of the Public Debt. As shown in the table, the weighted average duration of outstanding Treasury debt first fell from 3.9 years in December 2007 to 3.5 years in December 2008, after which it rose to 4.6 years in July 2014. This rise in maturity occurred alongside a dramatic increase in outstanding Treasury debt, which grew from \$4.5 trillion in December 2007 to \$12.2 trillion by July 2014.

To compare the increase in Treasury supply with the growth of the Federal Reserve's balance sheet, we again convert these quantities into ten-year duration equivalents. The adjustment has a large impact because the average duration of outstanding Treasuries is considerably shorter than the duration of the Federal Reserve portfolio, which disproportionately contains long-term bonds as a result of QE. Expressed in ten-year duration equivalents, the debt grew from \$2 trillion in December 2007 to \$6.3 trillion in July 2014. Thus, the total increase from 2007 was \$4,334 billion in 10-year equivalents, or 25 percent of GDP.

The growth in the quantity of ten-year duration equivalents issued by the Treasury reflects two forces: the expansion of the debt and maturity extension. More formally, we can decompose the change in ten-year duration equivalents into two terms:

$$\Delta\left(\frac{\text{Debt}_t \cdot Dur_t}{Dur_t^{10\text{-yr}}}\right) = \left(\frac{1}{Dur_t^{10\text{-yr}}}\right) \cdot \left(\underbrace{\Delta\text{Debt}_t Dur_{t-1}}_{\text{Debt Expansion}} + \underbrace{\Delta Dur_t \text{Debt}_t}_{\text{Maturity Extension}}\right) \quad (2\text{-}2)$$

The first term reflects the growth of the debt, holding constant the duration of the debt at its initial value. The second term captures the effects of the rise in the average duration. Since debt management policy plays almost no role in driving the short-term growth of the debt stock (which is driven by fiscal policies outside the control of debt managers), the second term captures the impact of active debt management policies.

This decomposition is shown in the last two columns of table 2-2. Roughly a quarter of the increase in ten-year equivalents was driven by the extension of maturity, with the remaining three-quarters driven by the expansion of the debt. Comparing panels A and B of table 2-2, we see that the Treasury's active maturity extension program offset 35 percent of the duration supply impact of QE, insofar as the proximate goal of QE was to reduce the amount of interest rate risk in private hands. More specifically, QE reduced the supply of ten-year duration equivalents by 15.6 percentage points of GDP, but the maturity extension increased the net supply of ten-year equivalents by 5.5 percentage points of GDP. Because of our choice of a 2007 baseline, these numbers are a conservative estimate of how much the Treasury's maturity extension offset QE; if we use December 2008 instead, 63 percent of QE was "canceled" by the Treasury's maturity extension. Irrespective of which baseline we use, when measured in ten-year equivalents, the *combined* effect of maturity extension and the increased debt stock far outpace QE.

The calculations we have just described are shown graphically in figure 2-1. Panel A shows the cumulative duration supply impact of the rising debt stock and the Treasury's maturity extension. Below the x-axis, we show the offsetting duration supply impact of QE, which the figure further breaks into Treasuries, agencies, and MBS. Units are in ten-year duration equivalents, scaled by GDP. Panel B shows the weighted average duration of Treasury debt, both taking account of and ignoring consolidation of the Federal Reserve and Treasury balance sheets.

Figure 2-2 provides a back-of-the-envelope estimate of the net impact on long-term yields by combining our duration supply estimates from table 2-2 and figure 2-1 with consensus estimates of the price impact of Fed asset purchases. Specifically, based on the meta-analysis in Williams (2014), we assume that a $600 billion large-scale asset purchase (corresponding to $397 billion ten-year duration equivalents) lowers the ten-year term premium by 20 basis points (bps). This suggests that the cumulative impact of QE has lowered the term premium by 137 bps ($= 20 \times [2{,}718 \div 397]$). At the same time, Treasury's active maturity extension has raised the term premium by 48 bps ($= 20 \times [962 \div 397]$), for a net reduction of 88 bps. While these calculations are crude, they capture the stark difference between Fed and Treasury debt management policy.[6]

---

6. Specifically, figure 2-2 assumes that the entire impact of LSAPs works through reductions in term premia, which is a simplification. Furthermore, it applies a constant price impact to these supply shocks. In practice, there are good reasons to think that the price impact of supply shifts may be diminishing and that there may be diminishing stimulative benefits to reducing term premia; see Stein (2012). However, there is little evidence on these scores.

FIGURE 2-1. Comparing Quantitative Easing and Treasury Maturity
Extension, 2007–14

Panel A: Ten-year equivalents, QE vs. Treasury maturity extension
Percent of GDP

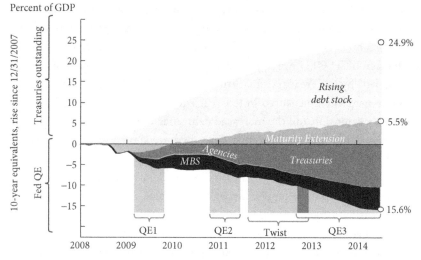

Panel B: Weighted average duration (WAD)
Years

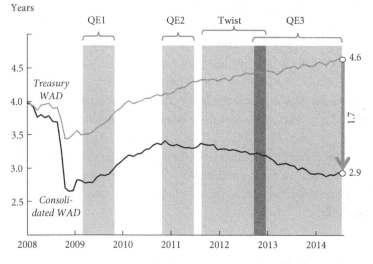

FIGURE 2-1. *Continued*

Sources: Authors' calculations using data from the Treasury's Monthly Statement of the Public Debt, the Federal Reserve System's H.4.1 Release (Factors Affecting Reserve Balances), and the Federal Reserve Bank of New York's System Open Market Account Holdings release.

Note: Panel A presents the cumulative change in ten-year equivalents (scaled as a percentage of GDP) associated with the respective balance sheet policies undertaken by the Federal Reserve and the Treasury. Positive values increase the interest rate risk placed in public hands (Treasury policies), while negative values decrease it (typically Fed QE, but also Treasury maturity shortening in 2008–09). Panel B presents the weighted average duration (WAD) of Treasury debt, as well as the WAD of the consolidated government debt position. The difference between the two lines is that Treasuries held by the Fed are excluded from the consolidated duration, and short-term interest-bearing Fed liabilities (excess reserves and reverse repos) are added.

This finding has both positive and normative implications. From a positive perspective, much has been made in recent years of the impact of QE not just on long-term yields (Gagnon and others 2011), but also on stock prices, exchange rates, and foreign asset prices.[7] A common view is that Fed asset purchases have a *mechanical* downward effect on long-term interest rates through the so-called portfolio balance channel. To the extent that QE is thought to operate through such a direct channel, the argument has to confront the reality that the totality of policy has *raised* rather than reduced the quantity of long-term government debt held by private investors. It is not consistent to believe—as some seem to—that QE primarily works through a direct price pressure effect that reduces yields, but that the crowding-out effect of large prospective deficits (which, of course, leads to increasing the quantity of government debt) can be largely neglected.

But if the direct supply effects of QE have been offset by the massive expansion in outstanding government debt and the Treasury's decision to extend the debt maturity, then what explains the large market impact of QE announcements documented in so many studies, as well as the fact that estimates of term premia on long-term bonds have been steadily driven

---

7. See, for instance, Neely (2012); Glick and Leduc (2013); Hooper, Slok, and Luzzetti (2013); Bauer and Neely (2014); and Mamaysky (2014).

FIGURE 2-2. Estimating the Market Impact of QE and Treasury Extension

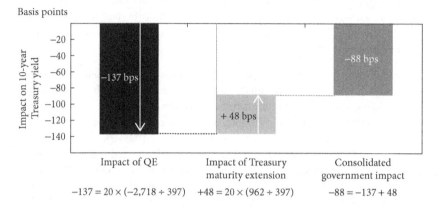

$-137 = 20 \times (-2{,}718 \div 397)$ $+48 = 20 \times (962 \div 397)$ $-88 = -137 + 48$

Source: Authors' calculations.

Note: The figure estimates the impact QE and Treasury maturity extension had on the ten-year Treasury term premium. The calculations are based on our ten-year duration equivalents in table 2-2, as well as the price-impact estimates in Williams (2014). Williams summarizes results from a large number of research papers that differ in methodology and data, finding a central tendency that a $600 billion bond purchase lowers the ten-year yield by fifteen to twenty-five basis points. To convert this $600 billion face value into ten-year equivalents, we assume bond purchases with a duration of 5.86 years and a ten-year bond duration of 8.84 years. The result is that $600 billion equates to $397 billion of ten-year equivalents. Using the Williams price-impact estimates, we reach an impact on the term premium of twenty basis points.

into negative territory and remain miniscule today, as shown in figure 2-3? The most natural explanation is that the Fed's announcements about its intended asset purchases also conveyed information about its future policies, including both the likely path of future short-term rates and the Fed's willingness to undertake further asset purchases in response to evolving economic conditions.[8] Furthermore, as Stein (2013) argues, there are good reasons to

8. There is strong evidence that the Fed's LSAP announcements moved the expectations component of long-term interest rates by essentially serving as an implicit form of forward guidance about the path of future short-term interest rates. See, for example, Krishnamurthy and Vissing-Jorgenson (2011, 2013) and Bauer and Rudebusch (2014). However, we are skeptical of the view that Fed has used LSAPs in an attempt to *credibly commit* to keeping short rates lower for longer than it other-

think that the Fed's announcements and its accommodative policies may have lowered the term premium on long-term bonds through a number of more indirect channels.[9]

Carrying this logic further, there are reasons to think that announcements of Fed asset purchases may have a greater impact on term premia than comparably sized Treasury supply announcements. Consistent with this, Rudolph (2014) provides event-study evidence suggesting that Fed announcements have about twice the impact as Treasury announcements of a similar size. Rudolph's analysis is reproduced in figure 2-4. Specifically, the figure shows the daily change in the estimated ten-year term premium based on the Kim and Wright (2005) model in response to Treasury's quarterly refunding announcement. The estimated term premium rose by 25 bps cumulatively over the five quarterly refunding dates when the Treasury clarified its intention to extend the average maturity of the debt. As noted previously, this is only half of the price impact (+48 bps) that one would have anticipated based on an extrapolation of large-scale asset purchase (LSAP) price impacts.[10]

---

wise might because, say, the Fed is concerned with maintaining a certain level of remittances to Treasury. Indeed, the Fed has repeatedly emphasized that the future evolution of short-term rates will not be limited by the elevated size of its balance sheet and its large holdings of long-term bonds. Nonetheless, Gagnon and others (2011) have used model-based estimates to argue that movements in term premia explain the vast majority of the announcement effect on ten-year yields. However, Bauer and Rudebusch (2014) are skeptical about the ability of such models to accurately disentangle term premia from expected short rates.

9. In particular, the Fed's policies may have boosted investor demand for long-term bonds *holding fixed* the expected path of short-term rates. First, the expectation that the Fed would "do whatever it takes" using both conventional and unconventional measures may have lowered the perceived risk of investing in long-term bonds going forward. Second, a decline in interest rates may boost the demand for long-term bonds from investors who want to maintain the current yield on their portfolios (Hanson and Stein 2015). If such a demand "recruitment channel" is operative, it means that the Fed's total impact on long-term yields may exceed the effect of any forward guidance on the expectations component and the direct effect of asset purchases on term premia (Stein 2013).

10. An alternative interpretation is that Fed asset purchases and Treasury supply changes have the same price impact, but that it is easier for investors to predict the evolution of Treasury supply than Fed purchases. As a result, much of the supply "news" released on quarterly refundings may already be reflected in term premia. In contrast, investors may have been more surprised by the Fed's LSAP announcements, leading to larger announcement effects.

FIGURE 2-3. Estimated Term Premia on Long-Term Bonds

Panel A: Term premium on ten-year zero-coupon Treasuries (1990–2014)

Percent

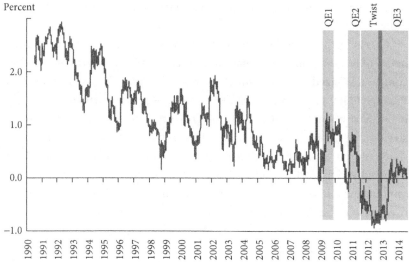

Panel B: Term premium on ten-year zero-coupon Treasuries (2008–14)

Percent

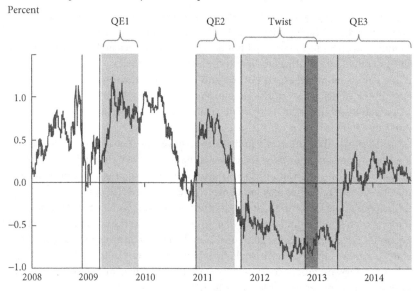

Source: Updated Kim and Wright (2005) data from the Federal Reserve.

Note: This figure shows estimates of the term premium on ten-year zero-coupon Treasuries based on the Kim and Wright (2005) model. This model decomposes long-term yields into an "expectations component" that reflects the expected short-term interest rate over time plus a "term premium" that investors require for bearing the interest rate risk associated with long-term bonds. Major QE announcements are marked by lines in panel B.

FIGURE 2-4. Event Study: Impact of Treasury Refunding Announcements on Term Premia

Panel A: Weighted average maturity (WAM) of marketable Treasury securities
Years

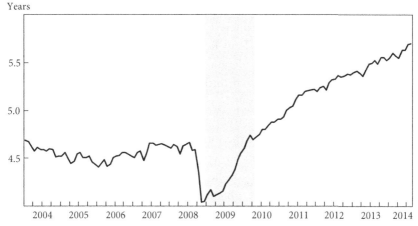

Panel B: Impact of Treasury refunding announcements on 10-year term premia
Basis points

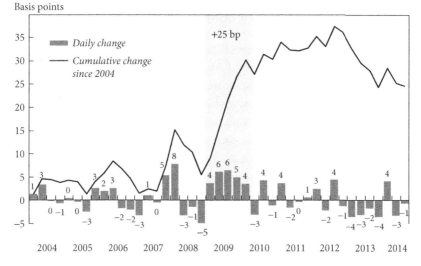

Sources: WAM data and refunding dates are from the Treasury. Term premium estimates are from Kim and Wright (2005).

Note: Panel A shows the weighted average maturity (WAM) of marketable Treasury debt over the past decade. Panel B adds up the daily and cumulative changes in the ten-year term premium on days when the Treasury's quarterly refunding announcements were released. Shaded in both panels are the five quarters when the Treasury was telegraphing its intent to extend the average maturity of the debt in its refunding announcements.

Nonetheless, from a normative perspective it seems very odd that the Federal Reserve is taking actions that have the effect of substantially reducing the duration of the debt held by the public at a time when the Treasury is arguing that it is in taxpayers' interest to extend the duration of the debt at a rapid pace. Moreover, the Federal Reserve has done so without formally acknowledging any of the considerations invoked by the Treasury. Similarly, the Treasury is taking steps that in the judgment of the Fed are contractionary, while committing itself in general to expansion of demand as a principal policy (through its stimulus measures postcrisis) without ever addressing the concern about the possibly contractionary impact of debt management. In the next section we consider the merits of lengthening versus shortening the maturity of the public debt and address the question of the process by which a government committed to both democratic control over economic policy and an independent central bank should address this issue.

Precedents for Fed–Treasury Cooperation

Before the 2008–09 financial crisis, it was thought by academics and policymakers that the Federal Reserve's dual objectives of low inflation and full employment were not in conflict with those of debt managers at the U.S. Treasury, who sought to minimize the cost of managing the federal debt while limiting fiscal risk. This understanding reflected the reality that the Treasury and the Federal Reserve each could independently pursue their respective policy objectives without much formal coordination.

This has not always been the case. Prior to the late 1970s, coordination between the Treasury and the Federal Reserve was commonplace and can be seen in both official communications and the correlation between the balance sheet positions of the two agencies.

Historical Precedents

Figure 2-5 provides an historical perspective on the link between the Federal Reserve holdings of Treasury securities, expressed as a percentage of GDP, and the size of the overall public debt. Over our 1936–2013 sample,[11] the correlation

11. There is limited data on the maturity structure of Federal Reserve securities holdings prior to 1936.

between these two series is 66 percent, which mostly reflects central bank balance sheet growth during World War II and the Great Recession. Outside of these two large events, in the 1952–2007 period, the correlation between the size of the Fed's balance sheet and the ratio of debt-to-GDP is near zero.

Panels B and C show that there is little correlation between the maturity structure of federal debt and the maturity structure of Treasury holdings on the Fed's balance sheet. Although the figure shows periods when a lengthening maturity of outstanding Treasury debt was also associated with a maturity extension within the Fed's portfolio (e.g., 1995–2007), the overall correlation is zero. The most discernible variation in the time-series, apart from the postcrisis era (i.e., 2008–13), is the 1940–50 subperiod, when the Fed played an important role in facilitating the rapid growth in national borrowing during World War II.

From the long history of debt management, there are a few interesting episodes that suggest debt management can be better coordinated when the circumstances warrant. Consider first the cooperation between the Fed and Treasury on debt management during World War II. A few months after the United States entered World War II, and in the midst of a rapid increase in government spending, the Fed and the Treasury agreed to fix the entire yield curve of Treasury securities. Three-month bill yields were limited to 0.375 percent and bond yields were held at 2.5 percent. The Fed stood ready to buy or sell any amount of Treasury securities necessary to maintain this positively sloped yield curve.

Because long-term rates were fixed, bonds experienced almost no price volatility in the secondary market, a condition that made them more attractive to investors. But while such an increase in the appeal of long bonds might otherwise flatten the yield curve, the Fed had committed itself to enforce a positive slope. The result was that during World War II, private investors bought almost all of the notes and bonds issued by the Treasury, which left the Fed to buy almost all of the bills. This can be seen in panel A of figure 2-5, where the share of long-term Treasury securities on the Fed's balance sheet plummets. In short, the Federal Reserve and Treasury effectively agreed during World War II that financing the war was the main objective of debt management policy, and they coordinated with each other to reach this outcome. While the nature of the cooperation (the Federal Reserve was acting to support fiscal expansion) does not carry over to the current debate, the fact that they *could* cooperate closely on debt management does have implications for current policy.

FIGURE 2-5. Fed and Treasury Balance Sheets, 1936–2013

Panel A: Breakdown by maturity
Percent of portfolio

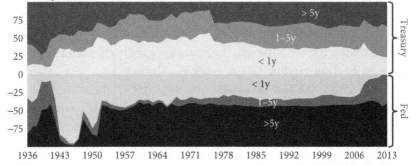

Panel B: Notional values
Percent of GDP

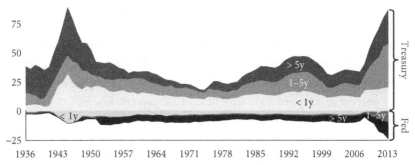

Panel C: Long-term debt share, Fed vs. Treasury
Long-term share/total

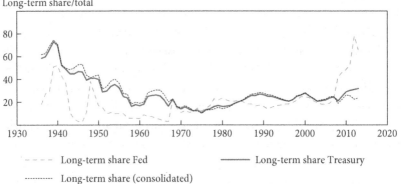

FIGURE 2-5. *Continued*

Sources: Data were compiled from various issues of the Monthly Statement of the Public Debt, *Treasury Bulletin*, Banking and Monetary Statistics, and *Federal Reserve Bulletin*.

Note: Outstanding balances of Federal Reserve (asset) and Treasury (liability) balance sheets are broken down into three buckets of remaining maturity: less than one year, one to five years, and greater than five years. Panel A shows this data expressed as a percentage of total Treasury assets (Fed) or Treasury liabilities (Treasury). In panel B, outstanding amounts are shown as a percentage of GDP. In panel C we show the long-term debt share, computed as the fraction of debt that is of five-year maturity or greater. The consolidated time-series nets out Federal Reserve holdings from Treasury liabilities.

Following the end of World War II, the Federal Reserve sought to assert independence by pushing for greater fluctuations in short-term interest rates. However, as the Treasury faced a large and growing debt burden, it maintained its pressure on the Fed until 1947 (Chandler 1966; Humpage 2014). In this way, monetary policy objectives were secondary to those of debt management. In 1947, the Treasury and Fed jointly agreed to a series of increases in the interest rate on short-term bills, which reached 1 percent in early 1948. This led some individuals and banks to sell their holdings of longer-maturity bonds. In response, the Fed began purchasing these longer-term securities while simultaneously selling an approximately equal value of short-term Treasury bills (Humpage 2014).

Tension between the Treasury and Fed reached a boiling point in January 1951, when the Treasury secretary publicly announced that maintaining a 2.5 percent yield on Treasury bonds was an "integral part of the financial structure of the country." The Federal Reserve, in a memo to President Harry S. Truman, stated that it did not agree with the directive. Following intervention by the president, the secretary of the Treasury and the chairman of the Federal Reserve released a joint statement in March 1951 that declared, "The Treasury and the Federal Reserve System have reached full accord with respect to debt-management and monetary policies to be pursued in furthering their common purpose to assure the successful financing of the Government's requirements and, at the same time, to minimize monetization of the public debt" (Hetzel and Leach 2001). This agreement restored greater independence to the Fed and became known as the 1951 Treasury–Federal Reserve Accord.

A second instance of cooperation—in fact, a series of repeated instances—occurred through the "even keeling" policy the Fed abided by in the years after the 1951 Accord. The Fed agreed to not alter monetary policy during the three-week periods when the Treasury was building up an order book for new debt issues in the primary market. Under the even keeling policy, the Fed would hold rates steady during Treasury offerings, thus avoiding disruptive changes that might endanger the success of the offering process. Wanting to limit the amount of time when monetary policy was unable to change, the Treasury began concentrating its issuance into four annual mid-quarter refundings (Garbade 2007). But overall, the even keeling process was meant to ensure that central bank objectives did not interfere with debt management.

The third and most prominent example of Fed and Treasury cooperation in the domain of debt management comes from the Operation Twist program of 1961. At the time, the Fed wanted to adopt a more accommodative policy but was reluctant to further reduce short-term interest rates because of concerns that this would impair the nation's balance of payments and result in gold outflows under the Bretton Woods system. In response, the Fed and Treasury tried to lower long-term interest rates by reducing the term premium on long-term bonds while holding short-term interest rates constant. Specifically, the Fed agreed to buy longer-term securities while the Treasury would sell predominantly short-term securities. Studies conducted shortly thereafter used quarterly interest rate data and found no meaningful impact of the 1961 program (Modigliani and Sutch 1966). However, more recent studies that make use of a modern event-study methodology have found a significant impact (Swanson 2011).[12]

Operation Twist is perhaps the best example of the potential for Fed and Treasury cooperation, because the circumstance was, much like the zero

---

12. Long-term interest rates fell on most dates in early 1961 when the initial information about Treasury and Fed policies was released. The only exception was when the Treasury surprised both the White House and the Fed by issuing longer-term bonds on March 15, 1961. This made James Tobin (then a member of Kennedy's CEA) "furious." Treasury continued to extend its maturity thereafter and within a year the average maturity had increased by 3.5 months (Swanson 2011, 203).

lower bound today, that the Fed was constrained in its use of the short rate as a policy instrument. However, unlike in the more recent period, during Operation Twist the Fed was able to complement its own actions with the secured cooperation of the Treasury to alter the maturity structure of new debt issuance.

International Precedents

Beyond the historical evidence of cooperation in the United States, another relevant benchmark is practice across the major economies.

Table 2-3 compares debt management practices across the Group of Seven (G-7) countries. The table highlights the wide variety of institutional arrangements adopted to coordinate debt management with monetary policy. In all countries in the G-7, debt management resides in the Treasury or a debt management office (DMO) controlled by the Treasury. While the comparison to Germany, France, and Italy is muddled by the fact that those countries do not have central banks that determine monetary policy, the experience of the other large countries is illustrative.

The table describes, in brief, the pre-2008 arrangement for coordinating debt management between the central bank and Treasury. The "QE era" column describes how debt management has evolved in the years since the financial crisis. The rightmost column lists the average debt maturity in 2014. Upon hitting the zero lower bound and venturing into QE, two different paths emerge for policy coordination. One alternative is shown by Japan and the United States, where debt managers extended maturity more aggressively than in any other G-7 country. Both countries lack any formal avenues for policy coordination between debt managers and central bankers. The other alternative is exemplified by the United Kingdom, where policymakers have a clearer record of coordinating debt management and monetary policy, perhaps because of the historical roles the Bank of England has played in both policy areas. The U.K. DMO is mandated to "ensure that debt management is consistent with the aims of monetary policy." As the Bank of England was getting ready to begin QE in early 2009, its governor sent a public letter to the chancellor of the Exchequer. The Bank of England claimed that in order to ensure consistency between debt management and monetary policy, the government should not alter its issuance strategy as a result of QE. The government confirmed that it would not alter its debt issuance strategy

Table 2-3. *Debt Management in the G7: Coordination between the Central Bank and Treasury*

Country	Pre-2008 debt management arrangement	QE era	Average maturity in 2014
United States	There are no formal institutional arrangements to coordinate with monetary policy. Treasury has full authority over U.S. debt management. The Fed tends to mimic Treasury issuance patterns and only target short rates (with some exceptions, such as World War II and 1961 Operation Twist).	Treasury extended its debt maturity to reduce rollover risk and catch up with other countries. The side effect was to counteract a portion of Fed's QE effects. It is not clear which agency controls the U.S. government maturity policy.	5.7 years
Canada	Debt management resides in the Ministry of Finance. The Canadian Finance Department formally consults with the Bank of Canada on debt management decisions and issuance schedules are announced on the Bank of Canada's website. In policy reports, there is discussion of the shared responsibilities and joint efforts of the Ministry and the Bank.	In the decade before the crisis, Canada's average maturity moved very slowly within a range of 6.0 years to 7.0 years. During the crisis, however, average maturity fell from 7.0 years in 2007 to 6.0 years in 2009, as bills were used to fund both fiscal deficits and the government's MBS purchase program. In 2012 the government announced that it would reallocate issuance toward long-term bonds to reduce refinancing risk.	6.0 years
France	There are no institutional arrangements to coordinate with monetary policy. In 2000, the Agence France Trésor was created within the Finance Ministry to manage the debt. The idea of an independent office was rejected on the grounds of democratic accountability and linkages to fiscal policy.	Maturity of French debt is currently at approximately the same level as it was in 2006 and 2007.	7.0 years

Germany	There are no institutional arrangements to coordinate with monetary policy. From 1997 to 2011, Germany's debt managers held the government's average maturity near 6.0 years. In 2001, debt management was taken out of the Finance Ministry and given to a private company to be wholly owned by the Finance Ministry.	In 2012, Germany's debt managers joined the international trend toward lengthening, increasing the average government debt maturity by nearly one full year since then (from 5.6 years in 2011 to 6.5 years in 2014). This has been the largest 3-year shift in Germany's average maturity seen in the past 15 years.	6.5 years
Italy	The Italian Treasury has the authority over debt management. However, the Bank of Italy advises the Treasury on debt management. In its advisory capacity, the Bank of Italy takes into account monetary conditions.	The average maturity of Italian government bonds has decreased by nearly one year since 2009. However, this may be due more to sovereign credit pressures than an attempt to ease monetary conditions. In 2014, the Italian Treasury has been trying to issue longer-term.	6.3 years
United Kingdom	In 1997, when the government gave the Bank of England independent control over interest rates, debt management policy was also taken out of the Bank of England to avoid any perceived conflicts with monetary policy. Debt management was assigned to the newly established U.K. Debt Management Office (DMO), an executive agency of Treasury. However, the DMO must "ensure that debt management is consistent with the aims of monetary policy."	As the Bank of England began its quantitative easing program in early 2009, the governor of the Bank of England sent a public letter to the chancellor of the Exchequer that in order to ensure consistency between debt management and monetary policy the government should not alter its issuance strategy in response to QE. The directive was accepted by the chancellor.	14.9 years

(continued)

Table 2-3. *Continued*

Country	Pre-2008 debt management arrangement	QE era	Average maturity in 2014
Japan	An office within the Ministry of Finance determines which maturities to issue, with a goal of ensuring smooth and cost-effective issuance. The central bank acts as fiscal agent but the Ministry announces all issuance plans and auction results. There is no special committee or working group to ensure coordination between debt management and monetary policy, despite both being actively involved in bond markets.	Bank of Japan has been engaged in a large quantitative easing program since 2010. Debt management since 2009 has been aggressively extending maturity to reduce rollover risk associated with large debt levels. The conflicting tactics of monetary policy and debt management are similar to the United States, except that in Japan, rollover risk may loom larger than refinancing risk.	7.7 years

Sources: Data compiled by authors from various sources, including the Organization for Economic Cooperation and Development (OECD); the International Monetary Fund (IMF) Fiscal Monitor; Sundararajan, Dattels, and Blommestein (1997); and national finance ministry websites.

based on the Bank of England's asset purchases. Indeed, the DMO shortened the average maturity by one year between March 2009 and March 2010.

The Optimal Division of Labor between Treasury and Fed

Given the target structure for the consolidated government debt, how should this be operationalized by the Fed and Treasury? And how should decision making authority shift—if at all—between the Treasury and the Fed as economic conditions change?

Optimal Debt Maturity and the Monetary Policy Cycle

In chapter 1 we described a series of trade-offs that the consolidated government must make to determine the maturity structure of the debt. For simplicity, our discussion treated these trade-offs as static in nature. However, if the trade-offs shift over time—leading to a time-varying optimal debt structure—who should be in charge? For instance, how should the government respond if heightened concerns about fiscal risk suggest a longer average maturity at the same time that a desire to bolster aggregate demand suggests a shorter average maturity? The consolidated debt maturity generated by independent Treasury and Fed action may differ substantially from the maturity structure that would result from a coordinated policy. Under the current arrangement, neither the Federal Reserve nor the Treasury is caused to view debt management on the basis of the overall national interest.

Table 2-4 describes the current division of labor between the Treasury and the Fed. Over the past thirty years, the two traditional objectives of debt management—achieving low-cost financing and minimizing fiscal risk—have been handled by Treasury. The two nontraditional objectives of modern debt management include managing aggregate demand and promoting financial stability. The former has been the exclusive domain of the Fed, while the latter has involved cooperation between the Fed and the Treasury, with the Fed taking a lead in bank regulation.[13]

13. For example, see the joint statement by the Federal Reserve and Treasury, "The Role of the Federal Reserve in Preserving Financial and Monetary Stability: Joint Statement by the Department of the Treasury and the Federal Reserve," news release, March 23, 2009.

Table 2-4. *Debt Management over the Monetary Policy Cycle*

		Traditional policy objectives	
		Achieving lowest cost financing	
Objectives and tactics	**Weight on objective**	??	
	Agency historically charged with objective	Treasury Department	
	Key market friction(s)	Investors derive money-like services from holding short-term debt	Long-term bond market partially segmented from other markets
	Main policy instrument	Fraction of debt that is very short-term	Weighted average duration of debt
	Normal implication for debt maturity	Issue more debt that is very short-term	Target a shorter average duration of debt
Conflicts driven by monetary policy	**Implications of contractionary monetary policy that raises short-term nominal rates**	→ Rise in premium on money-like assets → Increase amount of very short-term debt	
	Implications of recession where deficits rise and zero lower bound is reached	~	~

The columns list the four objectives of debt management as outlined in chapter 1: achieving lowest-cost financing, managing fiscal risk, managing aggregate demand, and promoting financial stability. For each objective, the table describes which agency is historically charged with the objective, the main policy instrument used to manage the objective, and the normal implication for debt maturity. The bottom rows consider two scenarios,

	Nontraditional policy objectives		
Managing fiscal risk	*Managing aggregate demand*	*Promoting financial stability*
??	??	??
Treasury Department	Federal Reserve	Federal Reserve
Convex costs of taxation, budget volatility costs, run-like problems	Long-term bond market partially segmented from other markets	Excessive maturity transformation by private intermediaries
Weighted average duration of debt	Weighted average duration of debt	Fraction of debt that is very short-term
Target a longer average duration of debt	Target a shorter average duration of debt	Issue more debt that is very short-term
→ None, assuming government executes a "barbell" strategy that holds average duration constant	→ None, assuming government executes a "barbell" strategy that holds average duration constant	→ Rise in premium on money-like assets → Increase amount of very short-term debt
→ Extend average duration since fiscal risk looms large	→ Shorten average duration to bolster aggregate demand	~

one expansionary and one contractionary, and the implications for debt management.

To tackle the question of who should be assigned responsibility over debt management (and whether this assignment should change with economic circumstances), we start by describing more precisely the circumstances in which debt management objectives, as they are currently interpreted by the

Treasury, conflict with the traditional output-inflation trade-off objectives of the central bank, and how easily this conflict can be overcome.

Conflict between the Fed and Treasury
Due to Variation in Liquidity Premia

Consider the stylized description of the monetary policy objectives embodied by the Taylor rule (Taylor 1993), in which the central bank raises interest rates when inflation is above target and lowers interest rates when output is below potential. Furthermore, suppose that the central bank uses the short-term interest rate as its only policy instrument. How might the optimal maturity structure of the consolidated debt be expected to vary over the monetary policy cycle, and how might this interact with the central bank's traditional objectives of promoting both full employment and stable prices?

Consider first the case in which the central bank raises interest rates to rein in aggregate demand to head off an incipient rise in inflation. With higher short-term rates, the opportunity cost of holding paper money and non-interest-bearing deposits increases, which in turn increases demand for money-like short-term debt such as Treasury bills (Nagel 2014). If the Treasury places weight on issuing "cheap" money-like securities to minimize the cost of the debt, the government should partially accommodate this greater demand by issuing more short-term T-bills. This motive may be further enhanced if the Treasury seeks to lean against the possibility that elevated demand for money-like debt may lead to excessive private liquidity transformation—that is, to avoid a surge in short-term debt issuance by financial intermediaries seeking to capture the heightened liquidity premium.

In this case, the conflict between the Fed and the Treasury arises because the Treasury's effort to shorten its debt results in unintended consequences from aggregate demand. As argued earlier, shortening the debt might reduce the duration-weighted supply of debt held by the public, thereby depressing the term premium component at long-term rates at precisely the same moment when the central bank is trying to tighten monetary policy.[14]

14. This assumes that expanding the supply of very short-term bills forces the Treasury to lower the average duration of the debt. However, as noted by Green-

Is there a way out in which both Treasury and central bank objectives could be accomplished without explicit coordination on debt management? In the case described, this could be accomplished by the central bank raising the short rate by more than it might otherwise have done, absent the Treasury's debt management response. Through this form of "sterilization"—although a strict second best to a joint decision on debt management—the central bank can undo aggregate demand consequences of debt management.

The opposite case—in which the central bank lowers rates while the Treasury lengthens debt maturity—poses more difficulty. If nominal interest rates are positive, then the central bank can sterilize a rise in the average maturity by lowering rates. However, if interest rates are at or near the zero lower bound, debt management limits the central bank's ability to pursue its traditional dual mandate.

Fed and Treasury Conflict Due to Changes
in Outstanding Government Debt

A second reason why optimal debt maturity may vary over the monetary policy cycle has to do with fiscal risk. When the debt rises as a percentage of GDP, the Treasury will prudently want to extend the average maturity of the debt to reduce refinancing risk. In ordinary circumstances, the debt-to-GDP ratio evolves slowly, reflecting the gradual accumulation of deficits or surpluses over time. During ordinary circumstances, we wouldn't expect the debt-to-GDP ratio—and thus the optimal maturity structure of the debt—to be tightly linked with monetary policy objectives, which vary more rapidly at a business cycle frequency. However, things are different when the economy enters a severe downturn, such as the United States experienced in 2009. In this case, increased fiscal expenditures result in a rapidly growing

---

wood, Hanson, and Stein (2015), one may be able to expand the supply of short-term bills while holding average duration roughly constant. For instance, to respond to the heightened demand for very short-term debt, the Treasury might increase its issuance of one- and three-month bills and reduce its issuance of six-month and one-year bills. At the same time, the Treasury could expand its issuance of two-year notes in order to hold the average duration constant. In this way, the government might be able to respond to the heightened demand for short-term money-like debt without depressing the term premium component of long-term yields.

debt stock, leading the Treasury to reevaluate the optimal maturity structure of its debt. At the same time, the central bank would like to aggressively use its conventional policy instrument to stimulate aggregate demand.

As we suggested before, the central bank can sterilize the impact of rising Treasury-led debt maturity through further reductions in the short-term rate. At the zero lower bound, this sterilization is impossible, but the Fed can still use its own balance sheet to undo whatever actions Treasury takes. For instance, if the Fed wants to reduce the supply of ten-year equivalents by $3 trillion to depress long-term rates and the Treasury's precautionary maturity extension raises the supply by $1 trillion, the Fed can simply perform an additional $1 trillion of QE to undo the Treasury's maturity extension. In other words, if the Fed is always the last mover, and the Fed has access to the same set of policy tools as the Treasury, it can always undo whatever the Treasury does.

Clearly, such a "solution" is problematic on many fronts. First, it puts all of the weight on the Fed's objective function and thus ignores the Treasury's fiscal motivation for increasing maturity in the first place. Second, it is a roundabout way of achieving the central bank's objective and adds an extra step of intermediation. If the central bank is free to choose the government's consolidated debt structure, then the Treasury should simply hand over the keys. Third, the Fed may already be constrained in its QE operations by the Federal Open Market Committee's (FOMC) perceptions about the size of its balance sheet, and in this case it makes no sense to further constrain the policy by forcing it to additionally undo Treasury action.[15]

The Optimal Division of Labor

To sum up, debt management may conflict with monetary policy objectives for two reasons. First, when the government alters the share of its debt that is short-term to react to shifts in money demand, this action may have implications for aggregate demand that differ from the Fed's objectives under its traditional dual mandate. Second, the set of circumstances in which fiscal

---

15. Rudebusch (2009) suggests that the $2 trillion Fed balance sheet in 2009 "only partially offset the funds rate shortfall." Relatedly, Rudolph (2014) argues that the Fed asset purchases would need to reduce long-term rates by 200 basis points to offset the shortfall implied by a standard Taylor rule.

risk looms large—leading the Treasury to lengthen the average maturity of the debt—are also circumstances in which the central bank faces the zero lower bound.

Where does that leave us? In the case of positive short-term interest rates, we favor an arrangement under which the central bank can manage the inflation output trade-off as it sees fit and can sterilize the aggregate demand impact of any policies that change the maturity composition of the debt using the short-term interest rate. Debt policy can be made by the Treasury on grounds of optimal public finance broadly understood to include financing the government at least cost over time, managing fiscal risk, and promoting financial stability. But because of the importance of debt management for the functioning of financial markets and because of its relation to financial stability, the Federal Reserve should have a more significant advisory role than it does currently.

If the central bank is able to sterilize the effects of debt management on aggregate demand using the short-term interest rate, then is there any reason for the Fed and Treasury to cooperate? Suppose that, following Treasury's decision on the maturity structure of the debt, the Fed can precisely fine-tune the short-term interest rate to achieve a desired level of aggregate demand. Absent cooperation on debt management, policy outcomes will be at second best, because they necessarily reflect the central bank's weights on the output-inflation trade-off over Treasury debt management objectives. More broadly, using two instruments sequentially to achieve four policy goals is inferior to choosing the two instruments simultaneously. This conclusion is further reinforced when we recognize that policy instruments map to policy outcomes with long and variable lags and with considerable uncertainty.

How do we see cooperation between the Fed and the Treasury occurring in practice? A natural solution would be for the Fed and the Treasury to annually release a joint statement on the strategy for managing the U.S. government's consolidated debt. This would establish a plan for the maturity structure and composition of debt issued by the Treasury and supported by the Federal Reserve. The Fed would be given the flexibility to make interim adjustments to debt management policy to engage in large-scale outright purchases or sales in response to economic or financial developments if such policies were needed to pursue its dual stabilization mandate. At the same time, annual coordination of this sort would make it unlikely that the Fed and the Treasury would be working at cross-purposes for long periods of time.

At the zero lower bound, this arrangement would cause the Treasury to internalize the Federal Reserve's desire to shorten maturity in order to stimulate aggregate demand. Similarly, the Federal Reserve would have to recognize the Treasury's precautionary fiscal motive for lengthening the maturity. In such situations a fully coordinated policy that the Treasury and Fed pursue with respect to currency intervention should be the norm.

There is also the question about which agency should accommodate shifts in the demand for money-like short-term debt that may arise over the business cycle as well as higher-frequency demand shifts due to "flight to quality" events. For instance, consider the large increase in demand for liquid short-term debt during the 2008–09 global financial crisis or during the fall 1998 crisis. Should such a demand shock be accommodated by the Treasury quickly issuing a large amount of bills? Or should it be accommodated by the Fed purchasing longer-term Treasuries financed either through an increase in interest-bearing reserves or reverse repurchase agreements (i.e., via Fed balance sheet expansion) or by selling T-bills (i.e., via an Operation Twist)?

Because Treasury bills, reverse repurchase (RRP) agreements with the Fed, and interest-bearing reserves are all very close substitutes, in principle either the Fed or the Treasury could take the lead in accommodating shifts in the demand for money-like short-term government debt. And regardless of whether the Treasury or Fed played the lead role, greater coordination is called for on this front since the Treasury and the Fed share responsibilities for promoting the stability of the financial system.

On balance, it seems most natural to delegate this role to the Fed because of its operational expertise in open market operations and its expertise in communicating with participants in funding markets.[16] In a sense, respond-

---

16. Blommestein and Turner (2012) reach a similar conclusion. Such high-frequency accommodation would likely pose significant operational challenges for the Treasury. For instance, it would be difficult to quickly contract the supply of bills in response to a change in market conditions (i.e., it would need to issue long-term notes or bonds to repurchase bills). In contrast, the Fed would simply contract the size of the SOMA by open market sales of long-term Treasuries, unwinding the associated RRP funding. It can also be argued that the Fed has a comparative advantage at managing any "rollover" risk associated with short-term debt: there cannot be a destabilizing "run" on the monetary base, but there could be a run on the T-bill market.

ing to shifts in the demand for money-like short-term debt is central banking in the classic sense of elastically supplying a special asset that supplies liquidity services and impacts financial stability. For instance, by using its RRP capability, the Fed could expand and contract the size of SOMA's holdings of long-term Treasuries backed by reverse repo funding in order to target a constant convenience premium on short-term money-like debt, which would be accomplished through standard open market operations. Of course, if this liquidity provision and financial stability role were delegated to the Federal Reserve it would likely need to maintain a balance sheet that was larger than its precrisis balance sheet.[17]

Summary

From 2008 to 2014, the U.S. Treasury deliberately worked to extend the average maturity of the consolidated public debt in order to limit the fiscal risk posed by the government's rapidly expanding debts. At the same time, the Federal Reserve actively worked to reduce the average maturity of the consolidated debt in order to lower long-term interest rates and, thereby, boost aggregate demand. Since both agencies use the same tool—the maturity structure of the net consolidated public debt—to achieve separate objectives, the nation faces an inescapable trade-off between these two conflicting policy goals.

Under current institutional arrangements, both the Federal Reserve and the U.S. Treasury tend to view debt management through the lens of each institution's narrow objectives and neither sets policy based on the overall national interest. We suggest new arrangements to promote greater cooperation between the Treasury and the Federal Reserve in setting debt management policy. Such coordination is especially important when conventional monetary policy reaches the zero lower bound, leaving debt management as one of the few policy tools to support aggregate demand.

17. Cochrane (2014) and Gagnon and Sack (2014) also argue in favor of maintaining a permanently larger Fed balance sheet in the new era with interest-bearing Fed liabilities.

COMMENT

Mary John Miller

From the perspective of a Treasury debt manager during most of the period covered in this chapter, as well as a former market participant, I would like to address three of the authors' recommendations: first, the addition of new mandates to traditional debt management policy; second, shifting debt issuance to short-term bills; and third, requiring coordination between the Treasury and the Federal Reserve over debt management policies.

The U.S. Treasury occupies a unique role in world markets, offering the deepest and most liquid securities market. The Treasury yield curve is considered the risk-free benchmark yield curve against which corporate, municipal, mortgage market, and even other sovereign issuers price their debt.

The authors assign little value to the risk-free benchmark yield curve and, in fact, seem to indicate that investors consume duration regardless of maturity, which suggests that simply buying more shorter-duration securities is the functional equivalent of fewer longer-duration securities. This is not in practice how it works. There is clear demand for securities of different maturities and durations, and the market plays a role in arbitraging opportunities across the yield curve.

The disciplined approach built by Treasury debt managers over decades results in low borrowing costs and liquidity premiums—the ability to finance at low cost because investors perceive a benefit to holding Treasuries versus other investments. The hallmark of this approach is telegraphing well in advance the size and frequency of borrowing needs, with any adjustments made with lots of notice. The decision to extend the average maturity of the debt post–financial crisis is a good example of this communication strategy. Despite adding longer-term supply, Treasury debt enjoyed higher coverage rates in auctions and lower premiums for longer-term debt during this period.

It is worth noting that compared to the G-7 debt issuers described in the chapter, the U.S. Treasury had the shortest weighted average maturity in

2014, even after five years of debt extension. Contrary to the impression that the chapter may create, the bulk of Treasury borrowing occurs at maturities of less than five years.

The economists' view represented in this chapter is concerned with managing aggregate demand in the economy and financial stability with the additional tool of debt management. Treasury is naturally more concerned with managing aggregate demand in the market for its securities as it seeks to finance the government at the lowest possible cost over time. It is one of the reasons that Treasury developed and issued new floating-rate debt during this period to address both the desire to issue term debt as well as the market's demand for highly liquid short-term securities. It is odd that the authors never mention Treasury's new floating-rate debt.

Treasury has no choice but to borrow; the Federal Reserve's purchases of long-term assets are discretionary. Even if deficits disappeared tomorrow, there is still an enormous stock of debt to refinance, not to mention the value of the Treasury market itself to investors.

The Fed's decisions to influence economic activity, such as with quantitative easing, can move markets with new information. If the Treasury were to adjust its borrowing around Fed announcements, this would fundamentally change the way markets view Treasury debt, likely introducing new uncertainty and borrowing costs. Rather than enjoying a liquidity premium, Treasury debt would assume a risk premium as the market awaited Fed meeting announcements regarding debt issuance. This seems entirely backward. The Treasury market should be a source of financial stability, not a contributor to excess volatility and uncertainty.

The chapter's premise that the taxpayers were harmed by a lack of coordination over debt management, that the Treasury's actions somehow tightened financial conditions beyond the level desired by the Federal Reserve, rests on big assumptions. If the Federal Reserve believed the Treasury's actions were reducing the impact of its purchase programs, it could have scaled up quantitative easing, akin to the proportion of other countries' programs, such as the United Kingdom and Japan.

The authors also argue for restructuring Treasury borrowing toward more short-term debt. While in most markets the yield curve is upward sloping—meaning it costs less to borrow in T-bills than thirty-year bonds—the absolute level of rates also matters. Over the past thirty years, ninety-day T-bill rates have normally been above the current thirty-year bond rate, meaning today's long-term financing costs are beneficial to the taxpayers.

The authors make a rather remarkable assumption that shifting all borrowing to the short end would not move short-term rates higher or increase volatility. In 2015, such a debt management strategy would mean rolling over more than $700 billion ninety-day T-bills each week—an extraordinary increase for the market to absorb.

No concern is expressed about rollover risk, the wear and tear of entering the market with such high volume and velocity, or even the possibility of a failed auction. Debt managers live in the real world of debt limit impasses with Congress and disasters like 9/11 and Hurricane Sandy that can raise very real issues about market access. A strategy that increases reliance on short-term funding for the government increases risk.

Finally, the chapter argues for a coordinated approach to debt management between the Treasury and the Fed and provides some historical examples for such an approach. Without delving into the details there is little evidence that coordination worked in the past. The 1951 Accord highlighted here was actually an agreement *not* to coordinate after a particularly contentious period. Similarly, the example of the 1961 Operation Twist exercise conducted by the Federal Reserve was undermined by the Treasury's issuance of long-term debt during that very operation. So history is not persuasive on these points. At a Brookings conference on this topic in September 2014, every commentator expressed reservations about disturbing the balance of current practice, although one indicated that there may be a role for such coordination in a crisis if the terms are agreed in advance.[18]

Ultimately, the authors support what exists today—strong communication between the Treasury and the Fed over debt management policy. The Federal Reserve is the fiscal agent for the Treasury and involved in every aspect of debt issuance. The allusions to conflict between these two great institutions that manage our country's fiscal and monetary policy do not square with my experience during this critical period.

18. For video and transcript of the 2014 event, see www.brookings.edu/events /2014/09/30-debt-management-quantitative-easing-treasury-fed.

COMMENT

Paul McCulley

This chapter is a rich contribution to the growing literature on the optimal monetary-fiscal policy mix in liquidity trap conditions. Our profession has for too long ignored this field of inquiry, presuming that Thomas Sargent was correct when he proclaimed that macroeconomic analysis and policymaking had advanced sufficiently to render study of liquidity trap exigencies to be of little usefulness.[19]

If only that were true! But it isn't, as evidenced by the harsh reality of liquidity traps in all major countries since the Minsky Moment of 2007–08. I am happy to be part of this burgeoning literature.[20]

I start with the proposition that Ben Bernanke was right when he poignantly argued, in 2003, with reference to Japan's self-evident liquidity trap:

> It is important to recognize that the role of an independent central bank is different in inflationary and deflationary environments. In the face of inflation, which is often associated with excessive monetization of government debt, the virtue of an independent central bank is its ability to say "no" to the government. With protracted deflation, however, excessive money creation is unlikely to be the problem, and a more cooperative stance on the part of the central bank may be called for. Under the current circumstances, greater cooperation for a time between the Bank of Japan and the fiscal authorities is in no way inconsistent with the independence of the central bank, any more than cooperation between two independent nations in pursuit of a common objective is inconsistent with the principle of national sovereignty.[21]

At that time, Mr. Bernanke was primarily preaching. After the Minsky Moment, as Fed chairman, he practiced his own preaching in extraordinary and courageous fashion. He led the Fed to use its powers to transfer

19. Sargent and Wallace (1981).
20. McCulley and Pozsar (2012, 2013).
21. Bernanke (2003).

interest rate duration risk from the private market to its own balance sheet—
essentially swapping newly created reserves of zero duration for long-dated
Treasury (and related agency) notes and bonds.

The Fed's maneuvers were not, it is important to stress, of the nature of a
"helicopter drop," as Bernanke discussed in 2002:

> In practice, the effectiveness of antideflation policy could be signifi-
> cantly enhanced by cooperation between the monetary and fiscal au-
> thorities. A broad-based tax cut, for example, accommodated by a
> program of open market purchases to alleviate any tendency for in-
> terest rates to increase, would almost certainly be an effective stimu-
> lant to consumption and hence to prices. . . . A money-financed tax
> cut is essentially equivalent to Milton Friedman's famous "helicopter
> drop" of money.[22]

And, in my view, it is regrettable that the Fed's massive balance sheet expansion in the half decade following the Minsky Moment was not explicitly
the result of an accord with the fiscal policy authority to pursue extraordinary, and sustained, fiscal expansion. Such explicit cooperation between the
monetary and fiscal authorities—which Bernanke advocated to Japan in 2002
and which now is being employed in that country—would have generated a
more robust, a more equitable, recovery than the one the Fed has been able
to nurture largely alone.

But near-religious belief in the doctrine of central bank independence in
our profession has served as a major obstacle to fruitful—even polite—debate
about a more optimal monetary-fiscal policy mix. The Fed was left to fight
the liquidity trap via asset price reflation grounded in exploiting what the late
Rudiger Dornbusch described as rational overshooting—namely, that prices
on Wall Street move much more quickly than prices on Main Street.[23] A key
aspect of this approach has been reducing long-term Treasury (and related
sovereign-backed) interest rates so as to reflate all long-dated (perpetual) private sector assets.

Thus, Greenwood, Hanson, Rudolph, and Summers are surely correct
that it makes no economic sense for monetary and fiscal authorities to act at
cross-purposes in the debt management arena when the explicit objective

22. Bernanke (2002).
23. McCulley (2014).

of the consolidated entity is to lower the yield of all long-duration assets. The implementation of this objective should be a technical matter,
regardless of one's view as to the wisdom of the government deciding to
pursue this objective. The authors provide a robust framework for addressing this implementation question. Status quo institutional arrangements
are clearly deficient.

The case for more closely coordinated monetary and fiscal policies, especially in liquidity trap circumstances, is clear at least to me. Yet it is fraught
with tension, in part because of the near-holy belief in strict central bank
independence within the macroeconomics profession. The technical matter of coordinated duration-risk management between the monetary and
fiscal authorities is a good reason for getting these matters out of the ca-
thedral. I applaud the authors of this chapter for furthering that cause.

COMMENT

Stephen G. Cecchetti

The quartet of Greenwood, Hanson, Rudolph, and Summers make two
very important contributions that analysts and policymakers should keep
in mind.

First, in thinking about the impact of government bonds on the real economy, consolidate the actions of the central bank and the fiscal authority.
So, if the purpose of policy is to change the duration of the publicly held
sovereign debt, focus on what is privately held. (There is a small and technical question of how to handle government agency debt. But that does not
obviate the authors' important observation.)

Second, assuming that debt managers are charged with financing their
governments at the lowest cost possible, they should be issuing shorter than
the U.S. Treasury typically does. The reason is pretty basic: the U.S. Treasury
yield curve normally slopes up and the volatility of the short-term rate is not
big enough to offset the advantage coming from this fact. This is something

debt managers in other countries seem to realize, as they often use interest rate swaps to reduce their duration exposure. That is, governments in some countries issue long in order to benefit from the liquidity premium that they receive for being the benchmark issuer, and then they swap short to avoid paying the term premium that comes from issuing long.

There are, however, two points in this chapter on which I disagree. First, the authors assert that the Treasury's preannounced and relatively mechanical lengthening of maturity to some extent neutralized the Federal Reserve's quantitative easing program. My disagreement comes from the fact that market participants clearly view the Federal Reserve as the marginal participant in the government bond market—and a big one at that. After all, it is hard to disagree with the fact that central banks can set the risk-free short-term interest rate without actually having to hold any bonds and without concern for the actions of their debt managers. So, I would argue that it was (and is) the central bank's actions that were setting the price and they can take full credit for the reduction in the term premium that we saw.

Second, the authors recommend that, in order to avoid conflict between the monetary policy and debt management policy, there should be increased coordination between the Fed and the Treasury. The authors are careful to note that in the past, the discussion of fiscal-monetary policy coordination was framed in the context of the former instructing the latter—that is, in terms of avoiding fiscal dominance and avoiding high levels of inflation that tend to accompany it. Their recommendation has causality running the other way: increasing coordination so that the fiscal authority would do what the monetary authority wants. They are primarily concerned with the effectiveness of policy at the zero lower interest rate bound.

That said, I question whether the creation of a coordination mechanism—something more formal than the regular dialogue currently in place—would serve us well in the long run. I worry that putting in place a governance structure that is designed to avoid conflict when the system is under stress would leave open the opportunity for abuse in normal times. If the Treasury is under some sort of obligation to follow the lead of the Federal Reserve in a financial crisis, why not the other way around during a budget crisis? My conclusion is that we should not change a system that works well almost every day so that it will work better once every few decades.

COMMENT

Jason Cummins

Greenwood, Hanson, Rudolph, and Summers argue that the Treasury and Federal Reserve should cooperate in managing the federal debt. At first glance, that seems perfectly reasonable. After all, what's the downside from cooperating to promote the common good?

The prima facie case comes from responses to the Great Recession, when it appeared the Treasury and Fed were operating at cross-purposes. Treasury was lengthening the average maturity of the federal debt while the Fed's asset purchases were shortening duration in an effort to stimulate the economy. One could argue, as the authors do, that Treasury blunted the impact of the Fed's program or at least made it so the Fed had to do more. At a minimum, the argument goes, one part of the government should have been working with the other part to achieve shared aims.

That sounds good in theory. What about in practice?

Unfortunately, a closer examination of the history of such cooperation suggests considerable room for skepticism, both in terms of the pluses and minuses.

To explore the negatives, go back to an earlier era of cooperation between the Treasury and the Fed. According to Robert Bremner in *Chairman of the Fed*,[24] Fed Chairman William McChesney Martin made certain the Johnson administration was "apprised about the thinking within the FOMC," the policymaking Federal Open Market Committee. That sounds like the kind of coordination Greenwood and others advocate.

In practice, such efforts were the precursor to the Great Inflation of the 1970s. In the fall of 1965, the Fed moved to raise rates after fifty-eight months of expansion. President Lyndon B. Johnson, always colorful in his delivery, said to Martin, "I'm scheduled to go into the hospital tomorrow for a gall bladder operation. You wouldn't raise the discount rate while I'm in the hospital, would you?"

Martin dutifully replied, "No, Mr. President, we'll wait until you get out of the hospital."

24. Bremner (2004).

Delaying monetary policy tightening for a gall bladder operation may seem trivial. But, LBJ went volcanic when Martin did raise rates: "How can I run the country and the government if I have to read on a news-service ticker that Bill Martin is going to run his own economy?" That comment captures the essence of the tension between the executive branch and the Fed—they won't always be able to easily agree to a joint statement on the strategy for managing the government's debt. Or, if they do, the risk is that one side becomes subordinate to the other.

Indeed, Martin was soon called down to the LBJ ranch to get dressed down for raising rates. The First Lady even got into the act when he arrived, saying, "I hope that you have examined your conscience." According to Bremner's account, Martin received the full LBJ treatment. The president asked the Secret Service to leave the room and then began pummeling the Fed chair, shoving him against the wall and saying, "Martin, my boys are dying in Vietnam, and you won't print the money I need." We know how the story unfolded from there: Martin did print the money LBJ needed, and economic performance suffered from the inflationary spiral that followed.

These examples are not unique. They occurred in the United States in every decade after World War II, until Fed Chairman Paul Volcker established the de facto independence of the Fed as an inflation-targeting central bank.

Turning to the other side of the ledger, let's examine the positives from cooperation. The authors say that Operation Twist—when the Treasury and Fed together tried to lower long-term interest rates while holding short-term rates constant—was perhaps the best example of the potential for working in concert. As it was recently when short-term rates hit zero, the Fed was constrained in the early 1960s in its use of the short rate as a policy instrument. The authors argue that during Operation Twist, in contrast to the recent period, the Fed was able to complement its own actions with the secured cooperation of the Treasury to alter the maturity structure of new debt issuance.

The authors cite Eric Swanson's[25] study of Operation Twist as having a "significant impact." Statistically significant, yes. Economically significant, perhaps not so much. Swanson finds that Operation Twist lowered long-term Treasury yields by a cumulative fifteen basis points over six possible events related to the program. Swanson concludes that this is a "nonnegligible easing in financial conditions." Reasonable people can come to different conclu-

25. Swanson (2011).

sions, but fifteen basis points of easing doesn't seem worth the very real risks apparent from other examples when such cooperation went wrong. If Operation Twist is the best we can hope for, then we should hope for better.

The international evidence is no more favorable. In fact, I came to the exact opposite conclusion as the authors with regard to the interaction between the Bank of England and the U.K. Debt Management Office. The authors argue that the United Kingdom pursued the right policy because there was explicit coordination between the Bank of England (BoE) and the DMO. However, that displays a very narrow understanding of the real reason for the coordination.

The BoE demanded that the U.K. DMO not alter its issuance strategy during QE. Why? Because the BoE gained its operational independence only recently in 1997 and wanted to keep it. To maintain its independence, it wanted assurances from the DMO that debt management wouldn't create any appearance that the BoE's QE was monetizing fiscal expenditures. Furthermore, the BoE is so concerned about maintaining its independence from the DMO that it has said it will eventually sell all its assets to ensure there's no perception of fiscal-monetary coordination. The conclusion from the U.K. experience reinforces the idea that a central bank has reason to worry about supposedly cooperative arrangements.

The central issue in the chapter is the perception—notice I don't say "proof," since there is none—that more cooperation during the Great Recession would have produced better outcomes. But if aggregate demand management is so important, when traditional monetary policy is constrained by the zero lower bound, the Fed can do more asset purchases and undo any aggregate demand negatives resulting from debt management.

The Fed's bond-buying, known as quantitative easing, could have been bigger. I see little reason why the balance sheet couldn't have gone to $5 trillion or more. The BoE's QE was larger as a percentage of GDP and so is the Bank of Japan's ongoing program. The authors argue that this is "second best," but there's no theoretical proof or empirical evidence to that effect. Indeed, one could make the opposite argument that separation between the Treasury and the Fed is a credible commitment to independent monetary policy, which is a good thing.

Finally, notice that none of the actual policymakers who lived through the Great Recession said that they were materially constrained by current Treasury–Fed practice. Chairman Ben Bernanke didn't complain that Treasury Secretary Timothy Geithner was undoing QE. And Secretary Geithner didn't complain that Chairman Bernanke was making U.S. debt somehow riskier by taking duration out of the market.

I have described the problems with the authors' plan, but suggested no alternative. As Geithner likes to say, "Plan beats no plan." So is there an alternative plan that might achieve some of the authors' goals? One possibility would be for the Treasury to follow more predictable policies in debt management. It might be straightforward for the Treasury to adopt policies that do no harm in extraordinary circumstances. For example, Treasury could commit to not lengthening the maturity of debt during or immediately after a crisis. As long as market participants trusted that the Treasury would eventually return to normal operating procedures, the imperative to do so immediately would be relaxed. Much as the central bank benefits from anchored inflation expectations, if market perceptions about the weighted average maturity of the debt were anchored, then the need to achieve them quickly— and potentially do damage or run at cross-purposes with monetary-policy easing—would diminish. In essence, policy reforms need not go as far as a compact between the Treasury and Fed in order to generate better outcomes.

In conclusion, Greenwood, Hanson, Rudolph, and Summers tackle important questions. Their chapter surfaces the key issues and offers some policy prescriptions for the failures they see. In particular, the Treasury and the Fed should cooperate on debt management based on the overall national interest. But generals always fight the last war, so while it may seem like Treasury–Fed aggregate demand management is a clever idea, we've tried it in the past and it has been responsible for some of our worst monetary policy mistakes. It would be truly dangerous for the Fed to sacrifice its independence in order to get some perceived additional bang-for-the-buck in certain situations.

References

Bauer, Michael D., and Christopher J. Neely. 2014. "International Channels of the Fed's Unconventional Monetary Policy," Working Paper 2012-028 (Federal Reserve Bank of St. Louis).

Bauer, Michael D., and Glenn D. Rudebusch. 2014. "The Signaling Channel for Federal Reserve Bond Purchases." *International Journal of Central Banking* 10, no. 3: 233–89.

Bernanke, Ben S. 2002. "Deflation: Making Sure 'It' Doesn't Happen Here," remarks before the National Economists Club, Washington, D.C., November 21 (www.federalreserve.gov/boarddocs/Speeches/2002/20021121/default.htm).

———. 2003. "Some Thoughts on Monetary Policy in Japan," remarks before the Japan Society of Monetary Economics, Tokyo, Japan, May 31 (www.federal reserve.gov/boarddocs/speeches/2003/20030531/).

Blommestein, H. J., and P. Turner. 2012. "Interactions between Sovereign Debt Management and Monetary Policy under Fiscal Dominance and Financial Instability," OECD Working Papers on Sovereign Borrowing and Public Debt Management 3 (Paris: Organization for Economic Cooperation and Development).

Bremner, Robert P. 2004. *Chairman of the Fed*. Yale University Press.

Chandler, Lester V. 1966. *The Economics of Money and Banking*. New York: Harper & Row.

Cochrane, John H. 2014. "Monetary Policy with Interest on Reserves," mimeo, September.

Gagnon, Joseph, Matthew Raskin, Julie Remache, and Brian Sack. 2011. "Large-Scale Asset Purchases by the Federal Reserve: Did They Work?" Federal Reserve Bank of New York Staff Report 441, March.

Gagnon, Joseph, and Brian Sack. 2014. "Monetary Policy with Abundant Liquidity: A New Operating Framework for the Fed," Policy Brief PB 14-4 (Washington, D.C.: Peterson Institute for International Economics).

Garbade, Kenneth D. 2007. "The Emergence of 'Regular and Predictable' as a Treasury Debt Management Strategy." Federal Reserve Bank of New York, *Economic Policy Review* 13, no. 1 (March): 53–71.

Glick, R., and S. Leduc. 2013. "Unconventional Monetary Policy and the Dollar," FRBSF Economic Letter 2013-09 (Federal Reserve Bank of San Francisco).

Greenwood, Robin, Samuel G. Hanson, and Gordon Liao. 2014. "Price Dynamics in Partially Segmented Markets," unpublished working paper.

Greenwood, Robin, Samuel G. Hanson, and Jeremy C. Stein. 2015. "A Comparative Advantage Approach to Government Debt Maturity." *Journal of Finance* 70: 1683–1722.

Greenwood, Robin, and Dimitri Vayanos. 2014. "Bond Supply and Excess Bond Returns." *Review of Financial Studies* 27, no. 3 (March): 663–713.

Hanson, Samuel G. 2014. "Mortgage Convexity." *Journal of Financial Economics* 113, no. 2 (August): 270–99.

Hanson, Samuel G., and Jeremy C. Stein. 2015. "Monetary Policy and Long-Term Real Rates." *Journal of Financial Economics* 115: 429–448.

Hetzel, Robert L., and Ralph F. Leach. 2001. "The Treasury–Fed Accord: A New Narrative Account." *Federal Reserve Bank of Richmond Economic Quarterly* 87, no. 1 (Winter): 33–55.

Hooper, Peter, Torsten Slok, and Matthew Luzzetti. 2013. "Impact of Fed QE on Global Markets." *Deutsche Bank Global Economics Perspective*, May 23.

Humpage, Owen F. 2014. "Independent within—not of—Government: The Emergence of the Federal Reserve as a Modern Central Bank," Working Paper 14-02 (Federal Reserve Bank of Cleveland).

Kim, Don, and Jonathan Wright. 2005. "An Arbitrage-Free Three-Factor Term Structure Model and the Recent Behavior of Long-Term Yields and Distant-Horizon Forward Rates," Finance and Economics Discussion Series 2005-33 (Board of Governors of the Federal Reserve System).

Krishnamurthy, Arvind, and Annette Vissing-Jorgensen. 2011. "The Effects of Quantitative Easing on Interest Rates: Channels and Implications for Policy." *Brookings Papers on Economic Activity* (Fall): 215-65.

———. 2012. "The Aggregate Demand for Treasury Debt." *Journal of Political Economy* 120, no. 2 (April): 233–67.

———. 2013. "The Ins and Outs of Large Scale Asset Purchases," Kansas City Federal Reserve Symposium on Global Dimensions of Unconventional Monetary Policy (www.kansascityfed.org/publicat/sympos/2013/2013Krishnamur thy.pdf).

Mamaysky, Harry. 2014. "The Time Horizon of Price Responses to Quantitative Easing," unpublished working paper.

McCulley, Paul. 2014. "Escape Fandango." *PIMCO Macro Perspectives*, September (www.pimco.com/en/insights/pages/escape-fandango.aspx).

McCulley, Paul, and Zoltan Pozsar. 2012. "Does Central Bank Independence Frustrate the Optimal Fiscal-Monetary Policy Mix in a Liquidity Trap?" Paper presented at the inaugural meeting of the Global Interdependence Center's Society of Fellows, Paris, France, March 26 (www.interdependence .org/wp-content/uploads/2012/03/Paul-McCulley-Fellows-Paper.pdf).

———. 2013. "Helicopter Money: Or How I Stopped Worrying and Love Fiscal-Monetary Cooperation." Global Interdependence Center's Society of Fellows, January (www.interdependence.org/wp-content/uploads/2013/01/Heli copter_Money_Final1.pdf).

Modigliani, Franco, and Richard Sutch. 1966. "Innovations in Interest Rate Policy." *American Economic Review* 56, no. 1/2 (March): 178–97.

Nagel, Stefan. 2014. "The Liquidity Premium of Near-Money Assets," NBER Working Paper 20265 (Cambridge, Mass.: National Bureau of Economic Research).

Neely, Christopher J. 2012. "Large-Scale Asset Purchases Had Large International Effects," Working Paper 2010-018 (Federal Reserve Bank of St. Louis).

Rudebusch, Glenn D. 2009. "The Fed's Monetary Policy Response to the Current Crisis," FRBSF Economic Letter 2009-17 (Federal Reserve Bank of San Francisco).

Rudolph, Joshua. 2014. "The Interaction between Government Debt Management and Monetary Policy: A Call to Develop a Debt Maturity Framework for the Zero Lower Bound," master's thesis, Harvard Kennedy School of Government, Harvard University.

Sargent, Thomas J., and Neil Wallace. 1981. "Some Unpleasant Monetarist Arithmetic." *Federal Reserve Bank of Minneapolis Quarterly Review* (Fall): 1–17 (www.minneapolisfed.org/research/qr/qr531.pdf).

Stein, Jeremy C. 2012. "Evaluating Large-Scale Asset Purchases," speech at the Brookings Institution, October 11 (www.federalreserve.gov/newsevents /speech/stein20121011a.htm).

————. 2013. "Yield-Oriented Investors and the Monetary Transmission Mechanism," speech at the Banking, Liquidity, and Monetary Policy Symposium sponsored by the Center for Financial Studies, Frankfurt, Germany, September 26 (www.federalreserve.gov/newsevents/speech/stein20130926a.htm).

Sundararajan, Vasudevan, Peter Dattels, and H. J. Blommestein. 1997. *Coordinating Public Debt and Monetary Management*. Washington, D.C.: International Monetary Fund.

Swanson, Eric. 2011. "Let's Twist Again: A High-Frequency Event Study Analysis of Operation Twist and Its Implications for QE2." *Brookings Papers on Economic Activity* (Spring): 151–207.

Taylor, John. 1993. "Discretion versus Policy Rules in Practice." *Carnegie-Rochester Conference Series on Public Policy* 39: 195–214.

Vayanos, Dimitri, and Jean-Luc Vila. 2009. "A Preferred-Habitat Model of the Term Structure of Interest Rates," Discussion Paper 641 (Financial Markets Group, London School of Economics and Political Science).

Williams, John C. 2014. "Monetary Policy at the Zero Lower Bound: Putting Theory into Practice." Brookings Institution, January 25.

3

A NEW STRUCTURE FOR U.S. FEDERAL DEBT

John H. Cochrane

What securities should the U.S. Treasury offer? Traditionally, the Treasury has offered long-term coupon bonds, short-term notes and bills, and retail savings bonds, securities not much changed since the nineteenth century.

But Treasury debt has taken on new and different functions in our financial system and in monetary and fiscal policy. Short-term debt has become a form of interest-paying electronic money, and all Treasury debt is widely used as liquid collateral.

Underlying these changes, financial, communications, and information technology have changed rapidly. The securities that financed Treasury borrowing and served financial markets decades ago are not obviously optimal today.

Furthermore, though we are currently experiencing a quiet time of great demand for U.S. Treasury debt, a strong dollar, and low interest rates, we also live in a time of large debt and doubts about the long-term ability of

I thank Effi Benmelech, Michael Boskin, John Campbell, Don Kohn, Sebastian Di Tella, Darrell Duffie, Niall Ferguson, Bob Hall, Derek Kaufman, Josh Rauh, Larry Summers, John Taylor, Luis Viceira, and participants at the U.S. Treasury 2014 Roundtable on Treasury Markets and Debt Management for many helpful comments.

the U.S. and other governments to pay those debts. Unexpected events such as a war, recession, or a new financial crisis will put pressure on the U.S. budget and borrowing capacity. An improved structure of Treasury debt can contribute to the ability of the United States to meet these challenges.

Finally, economic understanding of government debt has advanced in the last several decades, both through advances in economic theory and via the experience of policy innovations and events around the world.

The Treasury has already pursued several innovations, including inflation-protected securities and floating-rate notes. One can imagine many similar innovations and a more comprehensive approach.

For all these reasons, a ground-up reexamination of the structure of Treasury debt is important and timely.

Goals

The right structure of Treasury debt follows from the goals one sets for it as well as a recognition of the changed environment.

The first, traditional goal of debt management is to fund deficits at lowest long-run cost to the taxpayer.[1] Moreover, in times of war or economic emergency such as the recent financial crisis, the United States needs the ability to borrow additional amounts quickly and cheaply.

A second goal is to provide liquid and otherwise useful securities that the market desires—securities that enhance financial and macroeconomic stability, and securities that the government has a natural advantage in producing. To some extent, this goal is a consequence of the first. If the United States can issue securities that are more liquid, more useful, or otherwise more valuable to investors, then it will be able to borrow larger amounts at lower rates.

But this second goal has a direct policy purpose as well. U.S. Treasury debt has unique financial features and uses, deriving ultimately from the fact that U.S. debt is uniquely liquid and much less likely to default than any private debt. Providing the right structure and quantity of Treasury debt therefore has an economic policy benefit unrelated to financing deficits.

---

1. For example, the first item in the Bureau of the Public Debt Strategic Plan is "Government financing at the lowest possible cost over time." U.S. Department of the Treasury, *Bureau of the Public Debt Strategic Plan, Fiscal Years 2009–2014*, p. 5 (http://publicdebt.treas.gov/whatwedo/bpdstrategicplan09-14.pdf).

By analogy, the government profits by printing money. But monetary policy is primarily devoted to inflation control and economic stabilization, not to maximizing seigniorage revenue. More generally, the government provides public goods that it has a unique ability to produce, such as roads, defense, measurement standards, and currency.

A third goal is to manage the risks of interest rate increases and other adverse events to the U. S. budget and to the economy. For example, if interest rates rise 5 percentage points back to historical norms, then Congress must either raise taxes, lower spending, or borrow an additional $650 billion per year, once the $13 trillion of publicly held debt rolls over. The longer the maturity of outstanding debt, the longer that day of fiscal reckoning is put off. But issuing long-term debt may be more expensive. It's not a trivial problem, as the analysis in chapter 1 attests. The debt can be structured to allow the Treasury to manage risks induced by interest rates, inflation, and other factors more quickly and flexibly.

Macroeconomic stabilization is a new fourth goal. For example, the Federal Reserve's quantitative easing program essentially shortened the maturity of Treasury debt in private hands and swapped mortgage debt for government debt in efforts to stimulate the economy. Whether or not one approves of that decision, it is useful to ask if there is a better set of tools for managing Treasury debt as economic policy.

The Securities

With these circumstances and goals in mind, I propose that Treasury debt should comprise the following securities. Later sections explain in detail how each type of debt works and meets common objections.

Fixed-Value Floating-Rate Debt

This debt has a fixed value of $1 and pays a floating overnight interest rate. It is electronically transferable and sold in arbitrary denominations. Such debt looks to an investor like a money-market fund or interest-paying reserves at the Fed. The Treasury allows investors to freely exchange this debt for bank reserves at the Fed and thus to bank accounts and to cash.

Fixed-value floating-rate debt is a technically small innovation relative to today's short-term bills and floating-rate debt, but one with important advantages for financial liquidity, stability, and economic efficiency.

This debt becomes electronic, interest-paying money. A transfer of fixed-value debt from one owner to another is the same as a wire transfer of Fed reserves, and that's what "money" *is* today. It is a riskless store of value, an asset with immediate liquidity.

Interest-paying electronic money has been the ideal of monetary economics for decades. When money does not pay interest, people needlessly economize on its use. Interest-paying money allows the economy to be satiated in liquidity, without danger of inflation or need of deflation.

Over the last few decades, our economy developed interest-paying electronic money in the form of interest-paying bank accounts, overnight repurchase agreements, auction-rate securities, prime money-market funds, short-term commercial paper, and so forth. However, this inside money proved susceptible to a run in the fall of 2008. Fixed-value floating-rate debt is default-free and therefore run-free in a way that the U.S. government is uniquely able to provide.

Nominal Perpetuities; Fixed-Coupon Debt

This debt pays a coupon of $1 per bond, forever. The Treasury auctions this debt as it auctions long-term Treasuries today, and the Treasury pays down or retires this debt by repurchasing it in a similar auction.

Currently, long-term debt pays a sequence of semiannual coupons and then a big principal. For example, a 4 percent thirty-year bond pays $2 every six months and then $100 in thirty years.

Perpetual Debt

Both fixed-value and fixed-coupon securities are *perpetual.* They have no maturity date. As a result, each form of debt is a single security. Newly issued debt is exactly the same security as the debt already outstanding.

By contrast, with the current structure, last year's thirty-year bond is this year's twenty-nine-year bond. It is a different security from this year's thirty-year bond. The debt is currently fragmented into 375 distinct securities (table 3-1), each with a total size of less than $50 billion. If these hundreds of issues are replaced by two uniform securities, each with trillions of dollars outstanding, the debt would become a good deal more liquid. Bid-ask spreads and other trading costs would decline, and price impact (how much prices go down if you try to buy or sell a large amount) would decline.

Fixed-value debt will be especially liquid. Current short-term Treasury notes, bills, and floaters suffer small price fluctuations, triggering tax and accounting costs as well as bid-ask spreads. With $1 fixed value, these securities have no capital gains or losses at all, and they can have no bid-ask spread.

Conventional debt also needs to be rolled over constantly. The Treasury sells new debt to pay off maturing principal. Potter (2015) reports that in 2014, the U.S. Treasury issued $7 trillion of new securities, about half of the publicly held debt, but only $630 billion was new borrowing. The rest paid off maturing old securities.

One may worry that a roll-over might fail, or that investors might demand very high rates to roll over debt as they did in the Greek crisis. Even if that worry is far-fetched, investors face the cost and nuisance of rolling over their investments, and investors together with the Treasury lose the dealer banks' bid-ask spread every time the debt is rolled over: $6,370 billion times even a small spread is a lot of money.

Perpetual debt never needs to be rolled over. Investors may revolt and cause a spike in interest rates. But they must take the initiative to do so. Investors never need to do anything to keep their positions going.

Though both kinds of debt are perpetual, one should think of fixed-value floating-rate debt as short-term debt and fixed-coupon, floating-value debt as long-term debt. Duration—the sensitivity of the value of debt to interest rate changes—is a better measure of short-term or long-term nature than is maturity. Fixed-value debt is completely insensitive to interest rates, just like overnight debt. Fixed-value debt is essentially overnight debt that is rolled over by default unless the investor does something about it. Fixed-coupon debt trades the certainty of coupons for short-term price fluctuations, just like today's long-term debt.

Treasury debt is only offered in large denominations, deliberately limiting its liquidity and use by retail investors. Currently Treasury bills, notes, and bonds can only be purchased in increments of $100. The standard economic justification is that this practice forces a separation between "money" and "bonds." That distinction is no longer relevant. The whole point of this proposal is to increase liquidity and financial usefulness of debt, to reduce the distinctions between "money" and "bonds." As a consequence, all Treasury debt should be sold in any increment, down to the penny.

Indexed Perpetuities

This debt pays a coupon of $1 times the current consumer price index (CPI). For example, the March 2015 CPI is 236.119—meaning, roughly, that a basket of goods costing $100 in 1982–84 costs $236.119 in March 2015. Then, indexed-debt coupons for March 2015 would pay $2.36119 rather than the $1.00 coupons of nominal perpetuities, on an annualized basis. As the CPI rises and falls, these coupons rise and fall.

Current Treasury inflation-protected securities (TIPS) have a complex inflation adjustment to coupon and principal. Like coupon bonds, each TIPS issue is a different security and thus small and illiquid. The illiquidity of TIPS was particularly apparent in wide price fluctuations during the financial crisis of 2008. My modified structure would again yield a single, simple, much more liquid security, with quantity outstanding above a trillion dollars.

The indexed perpetuity is the cornerstone risk-free investment of modern long-horizon portfolio theory. Economists thought TIPS would be more popular than they are. The complex structure of current TIPS may be holding them back. If so, a simplified security more closely aligned to its economic function should be popular.

Together, these features should result in a more popular security and improve the functioning of the financial system.

Tax-Free Debt

Treasury debt should be free of all income, estate, capital gains, and other taxes.

Optimal taxation principles say not to tax rates of return. These principles are honored a bit in the United States with a complicated system of tax shelters and preferences. Tax-free Treasury debt would be a lot simpler and save a lot of lawyer and accountant fees. It would be a very popular security, again allowing the Treasury to sell more at lower rates.

Taxing the interest on debt makes it seem that the Treasury pays less interest net of taxes. But investors who must pay taxes on interest offer less to purchase taxable debt in the first place. Therefore, in the first instance the Treasury gains nothing from interest taxation. In fact, the Treasury can lower interest costs by offering tax-free debt, since taxable investors will voluntarily pay the value of their tax-avoidance costs up front.

One may suspect that tax-free debt would be a present to high-tax investors. I demonstrate the opposite conclusion. High-tax investors don't have to buy Treasury debt in the first place and largely don't do so. Under plausible assumptions, then, offering tax-free debt would attract high-tax investors back to the Treasury market. It would remove a subsidy to *nontaxable* investors, such as pension funds, endowments, and foreign central banks, that enjoy high taxable interest rates without paying taxes.

Variable-Coupon Debt

Long-term debt should allow the government to temporarily lower coupons without triggering legal default.

This provision would help the U.S. government in times of extreme fiscal stress. Businesses in trouble cut dividends and then restore dividends when trouble has passed. I propose a structure similar to noncumulative preferred stock. The debt promises a coupon, $1 per share or $1 × CPI per share. That coupon can be cut and is promptly restored to the promised level as soon as possible.

The United States can cut coupons already. U.S. debt is not collateralized, and the U.S. cannot be taken to bankruptcy court. But cutting coupons or principal of current debt would trigger a legal default, which would be a mess. Bondholders could try to seize government assets, refuse tax payments, and sue. If nothing else, legal default would hobble the debt's eligibility as collateral, and many institutions would be forced to dump the debt by legal and accounting rules.

I contrast this proposal to various proposals for variable-coupon debt, including GDP-linked debt. I argue that this system provides more flexibility. GDP-linked debt can't adjust to a war, when GDP might increase, or to a financial or sovereign debt crisis, in which GDP might not measure well the government's financing need.

Swaps

The Treasury should manage the maturity structure of the debt, and the interest-rate and inflation exposure of the federal budget, by transacting in simple swaps among these securities.

Suppose that the Treasury wishes to increase the maturity of the debt. Rather than buy back trillions of short-term debt and issue new long-term debt, the Treasury could just enter a large swap of fixed for floating interest payments. Even small banks manage risk in this way.

Swaps would also allow the Treasury to separate the liquidity provision, financial stability, and other economic policy goals of its debt management from its risk management goals. For example, the Treasury could issue lots of money-like fixed-value floaters to satisfy liquidity demand, but swap out the interest rate risk. The special liquidity demand for fixed-value debt attaches to the bond itself, not to its interest rate risk exposure.

The Treasury can offer a very simple swap contract. The security replicates borrowing a dollar at the floating rate to invest a dollar in fixed-coupon perpetuities. This simple contract is equivalent to a fixed-for-floating swap collateralized by floating-rate debt, with none of the contractual complexities of regular swaps. This swap contract should also be attractive to small businesses and homeowners desiring to manage interest rate risks but who are currently too small to access swap markets, or as the basis for intermediaries to offer similar products.

Limits

Why stop here? Markets demand all sorts of additional fixed-income products. It is better, however, for financial intermediaries to create the wide variety of products designed to meet specific and changing retail demands, backed or hedged in part by Treasury debt. That is the private sector's comparative advantage. The Treasury's unique ability is to provide nearly default-free and uniquely liquid debt.

I address economic questions. There are legal questions, too: How many of these changes could or should the Treasury undertake of its own accord, and how many need enabling legislation? There will also be political questions: Some businesses benefit from current Treasury debt structures and will object to changes. I do not limit analysis of economic possibilities by an amateurish analysis of current legal, accounting, or political limitations. In part, if we can agree on the economic desirability of a new debt structure, then the legal, accounting, and political landscape will change.

This chapter is informed by a long economic literature on optimal taxation, optimal maturity structure and state-contingency of government debt, monetary-fiscal policy coordination, sovereign default, and so forth. I do not tie the analysis to a particular model in this tradition, or to a particular model's recommendation for optimal debt management and monetary policy. My goal is to assemble the *tools* recommended by this literature, leaving just how and when to *use* those tools in the background. We can agree on the tools while disagreeing how best to use them. For example, we can agree that swaps are a desirable way to adjust the interest rate exposure of the debt without agreeing on whether now is a good time to go long or to go short.

Any paper on government debt should start with a nod to the Modigliani-Miller theorem. If markets are frictionless, if taxes are lump sum, and if representative agent conditions hold, then the structure of government debt is irrelevant. (Chapter 1 also discusses this point.) Any gains or losses the government makes on its bond portfolio are paid by the same taxpayers who hold the bonds.

My analysis is rooted in three particular failures of this theorem: (1) government bonds and money have important liquidity and collateral value in the financial system, (2) taxes distort, and (3) default and inflation are costly.

Now, let's look at each security in detail.

Fixed-Value Floating-Rate Debt

In place of short-term bills and notes, the U.S. Treasury should issue perpetual, fixed-value floating-rate, electronically transferable debt in arbitrary denominations. I need a sexy name. "Treasury electronic money" describes its function. "Fixed-value floaters" describes it as a debt instrument.

The value of this debt is always $1 per bond. That value is guaranteed by a Treasury commitment always to buy or sell such debt at a price of $1. If a bank delivers $1 of reserves to the Treasury, the Treasury issues one bond, and vice versa. If individuals or nonbank institutions want to buy or sell a bond, they direct their bank to deliver or receive reserves to the Treasury. To the investor, this Treasury debt then looks like a money-market fund, or interest-paying reserves at the Fed, and is instantly convertible to a bank account or cash. Reserves are freely convertible to cash, so the relative price of Treasury electronic money and cash is similarly fixed.

In addition, anyone also has the right to pay taxes or receive government payments directly to or from fixed-value debt. Tax payments made earlier than due receive interest at the Treasury floating rate.

At one level, there is little difference between the Treasury's commitment to accept maturing debt at face value for tax payments versus its commitment to exchange debt for reserves, the Fed's commitment to exchange reserves for currency, and the Treasury's commitment to accept currency and reserves for tax payments.

But the direct commitment is clearer, simpler, and stronger. It allows Treasury debt to operate as full-fledged electronic money independently of banks and the Federal Reserve. Fundamentally, interest-paying money gains its value by the government's commitment to accept that money at face value for tax payments, not by its scarcity. (For example, see Cochrane 2005, 2014b.) I'll take your Treasury debt in exchange for an economics lecture, if I know that I can use that debt to pay taxes or sell it to someone else who has that need. The Fed might change who can hold reserves or other terms of their use. Banks and bank reserves might fade away in an electronic payments economy. When considering the legal definition of a security that will last forever, a backstop direct grounding of that security's definition and value, independent of current monetary arrangements, is desirable.

The floating rate is paid daily by incrementing the number of bonds in the investor's account. The full equivalence of fixed-value debt with reserves means there is no reason to daily send reserves to a separate bondholder's bank account.

Setting the Floating Rate

The Treasury has the legal right to set the floating rate as it wishes. The legal right in this security is the right to a $1 value, to exchange the security for $1 of reserves and hence currency at any time, and to extinguish $1 of tax liability by its surrender. This right to leave at any moment, not an interest rate formula, guarantees the investor's subsequent rate of return.

Within the legal right to set the floating rate, however, the Treasury will need a policy. That policy may change over time as the financial environment changes.

In the current environment, it is natural for the Treasury to benchmark the floating rate to the interest that banks receive on reserves at the Federal Reserve. Banks are then indifferent to the two assets. The Treasury can manage the amount of floating-rate debt outstanding by offering a few basis points more or less than interest on reserves to attract or to discourage investors.

A policy of benchmarking to interest on reserves also makes clear the intent of this security: to offer the same security as banks have at the

Fed—electronically transferable interest-paying money—to the general public. And it clearly preserves the understanding that the Fed is in charge of short-term interest rate policy. The interest-rate ship sails more smoothly with one captain.

That policy, however, presumes that the Fed maintains its currently envisioned operating procedures, consisting of abundant excess reserves, paying interest on reserves within basis points of market rates, and using interest on reserves as the policy instrument. If the Fed goes back to a small amount of non-interest-bearing reserves, the Treasury will have to set its own rate.

The Treasury could benchmark the rate to an index of market rates, including the federal funds rate, repo rates, or Libor rates, as well as the Fed's interest rate on reserves. The Treasury could set the rate directly as a policy tool, as the Fed sets interest on reserves.

The Treasury could also conduct daily auctions to reset the rate. The price is fixed at $1, but the Treasury can take bids for how much investors want to buy and sell at each possible interest rate. Market orders specify a quantity at any rate. The interest rate paid to all investors is the one that clears the daily market. The Treasury can sell or repurchase debt via a market order or a sloping set of orders, or it can run a corridor system, with small market orders and large bid and ask orders separated by a spread. That system would allow the rate to respond to market forces inside a band. Many central banks operate such a system.

The main difference between all these alternatives is how much the Treasury wishes to control day-to-day variation in the floating rate versus variation in the relative quantity of Fed reserves and Treasury debt. The total quantity of reserves plus debt held by the public remains fixed. It is, again, a largely technical issue not essential to the security.

Why?

Economists have long dreamed of interest-paying money. It fulfills Milton Friedman's (1969) optimal quantity of money without inflation or deflation. Money, either paper or electronic, is essentially free to produce, so the economy should be satiated in the liquidity that money provides. Financial arrangements designed to save on the lost interest of holding money are a social waste. The economy gains the area under the money demand curve, which Lucas (2003) estimated as at least 1 percent of GDP. Electronic money is particularly attractive in allowing very low cost, secure transactions.

More important, interest-paying Treasury money benefits financial stability. Our economy invented interest-paying electronic money in the form of money-market funds, overnight repurchase agreements, and short-term commercial paper, and found it useful. But that inside money failed, suffering a run in the 2008 financial crisis. Treasury-provided, interest-paying electronic money is immune from conventional runs. (For more, see Cochrane 2014b.)

Providing money is a key government responsibility. In the nineteenth century, the Treasury provided coins. Printing advances allowed for paper money, and banks issued notes. Notes were convenient, being a lot lighter than coins. But there were repeated runs and crises involving bank notes. Late in the nineteenth century, the U.S. government issued paper money, which might inflate, but cannot suffer conventional default or a run. That money eventually drove out private banknotes and that source of financial crises ended. (Crises involving demand deposits did not end, but here the United States tried a different policy response, deposit insurance and risk regulation, which has not worked as well.)

In the twenty-first century, following the revolutions in communications, calculation, and financial engineering that make interest-paying money possible, the Treasury has the same natural monopoly in providing default-free and run-free interest-paying money.

Treasury debt is already liquid and "money-like," and the Treasury already realizes this function in its issuance strategy.[2] Fixed-value, electronically transferable floating-rate debt will be even more liquid and desirable than short-term bills and current floaters. Its bid-ask spread will be set entirely by technological limitations—how much the Treasury charges for changing bits in its computers, which could be zero. You can't have asymmetric information or price pressure of a fixed-value security. The market depth will be several trillions, rather than the tens of billions of typical Treasury bill issues. It can be more liquid even than bank reserves, since anyone can hold Treasury debt but only banks can hold reserves. Recent short-term Treasury interest rates persistently below interest on reserves are evidence that such liquidity inversion is possible.

The Treasury should facilitate electronic transactions in this fixed-value debt. Its existing services such as Treasury Direct, Direct Express, and Pay.gov are an important foundation. Exchange and settling via Treasury accounts

2. See "Treasury Plans More Short-Term Debt" (www.wsj.com/articles/treasury-plans-more-short-term-debt-1430966689).

can be handled among financial institutions just as Fedwire handles the exchange of reserves and current Treasury debt.

However, the Treasury does not necessarily have a comparative advantage in the design and operation of large-volume, low-cost secure transactions services, especially ones open to retail customers. An industry of money-market funds and electronic exchanges, as well as banks, should be allowed and encouraged to offer transactions services accounts in or backed by fixed-value Treasuries. I should be able to buy a cup of coffee by bumping a cell phone and transferring $1.53 of an account consisting of or backed 100 percent by fixed-value Treasuries, and paying something like Bitcoin's minuscule transactions fees rather than the 4 percent fee charged by credit card companies.

The carrot: If fully invested in fixed-value Treasuries and walled off from bankruptcy of related or sponsoring financial institutions, such intermediaries need no risk regulation. They are as un-"systemic" as a financial institution can be. The only cause for regulation is to ensure against fraud.

The Treasury already offers floating-rate debt in addition to short-term Treasury bills. Current floaters have a two-year maturity. They pay the same rate as thirteen-week bills. Though frequent rate resetting typically results in small variation in market value, their market values do vary. This variation triggers capital gains taxes, which are absent in a fixed-value security. And the nature of the index matters to investors in the absence of the fixed-value guarantee.

In one sense, then, fixed-value floaters are just a small improvement on the short-term and floating treasury debt that we already have. This fact should allay fears that the final step will open a Pandora's box of unintended consequences. On the other hand, the small changes—removing the fixed maturity, fully fixing the price at $1—will quite substantially increase the liquidity and value of the securities as true "electronic money."

Why Not the Fed?

The same economic benefits could be achieved if the Federal Reserve were to open interest-paying reserve accounts to the general public. The Fed would likely have to increase substantially the size of its balance sheet, buying up Treasury short-term debt to issue such reserves.

However, the Fed is a central bank and by tradition and law only transacts with banks or other large financial institutions. Offering accounts directly to the public requires a big institutional and legal change.

By contrast, the Treasury already sells to the public. If people can buy bonds from the Treasury web page, why not a "bond" that happens to work just like a money-market account? The Treasury has provided currency. Why not currency that pays interest?

In sum, a technically small modification of existing Treasury securities, easily within the Treasury's legal authority and traditional scope of operation, is an easier institutional path than modifying the Fed's legal authority and scope of operations.

Monetary Policy and Price-Level Determination

How is the price level determined? The traditional story is that people hold bonds for saving and non-interest-paying money for quick liquidity and to make transactions. The Fed controls the price level by controlling the quantity of money relative to bonds—that is, the split of government liabilities between interest-paying and non-interest-paying flavors.

Fixed-value floating-rate, electronically transferable Treasury debt, held in large quantities so that we are satiated in liquidity, eliminates what is left of the rapidly vanishing distinction between "money" and "bonds." An account held for savings purposes happens to function as excellent money. Nobody must forgo interest in order to hold liquid assets. Must we eschew these benefits and hobble Treasury debt for price-level control?

No. We crossed that Rubicon long ago. The Federal Reserve's large balance sheet and interest-paying excess reserves undid the classic tale of price-level control. Private interest-paying electronic money in the form of interest-paying checking accounts, money-market funds, overnight repo, commercial paper, auction-rate securities, and so forth undid that tale. The fact that banks long ago started getting most of their funds from liabilities that do not require reserves, and the fact that the Fed stopped pretending to target monetary aggregates, fixing interest rates instead and letting the quantity of money be whatever is desired at that rate, undid that tale.

Monetary theory is now based entirely on interest rate targets, not the rationing of non-interest-bearing cash or inside money. Thirty years' experience of stable inflation with no control at all of monetary aggregates and despite the spread of interest-paying money confirms the modern theory. If banks can have interest-paying reserves and wholesale funding, if financial institutions can have a large shadow-banking system, and if the Treasury can offer short-term debt so liquid it pays a lower rate than bank reserves, all without undermining price-level control, the minor extension of floaters and bills to fixed-value debt will not have a dramatic effect. (Woodford 2004 is the standard summary of price-level control with interest rate targets in modern macroeconomic models. Cochrane 2014c offers an even simpler view based on the fiscal foundations of money, which does not require a Taylor rule.)

A second worry is that this system might undermine the Fed's ability to control the size of bank reserves. Such control is less important if the Fed sets interest on reserves equal to the market rate and maintains a large balance sheet. But such control may be more important if the Fed decides to revert to a small quantity of reserves that do not pay interest and to control short-term interest rates, and bank lending and deposits, by altering the quantity of reserves. If everyone has the right to convert Treasury floaters to reserves, will that not imply huge variation in reserves?

If the Treasury decides to tightly control the quantity of short-term debt outstanding, as it does now, there is no problem. Though each individual can obtain reserves (or deposits, by directing reserves to that individual's bank), the aggregate quantity of reserves cannot change if the aggregate quantity of Treasury floaters does not change. The Treasury would run a daily auction to determine the interest rate, and rate variation would clear the market at a fixed supply.

If the Treasury sets a fixed rate, or a sloping supply curve, and lets the quantity of floaters fluctuate, then to keep the overall quantity of debt constant, the Treasury must offset smaller numbers of floaters with larger amounts of other debt, and vice versa. Mechanically, if investors want $1 billion of floaters exchanged for reserves, the Treasury transfers $1 billion from its reserve account at the Fed to the reserve accounts of the investor's banks. Then, the Treasury must sell $1 billion of other securities to replenish its reserve account, which will automatically drain the reserves from the banking system.

More generally, the Federal Reserve is adept at offsetting reserve fluctuations induced by Treasury auctions. Fluctuations induced by net demand for floaters should not pose a grave problem. The Fed can undo by open market operations any change in reserves. The Fed can easily buy and sell floaters and so control the quantity of reserves instantly and precisely.

Credit

A common objection is that banks need to offer fixed-value deposits in order to supply credit to the economy. If the Treasury offers attractive fixed-value deposits instead, banks will be deprived of a key source of funds and will not be able to offer enough credit.

The simple form of this argument falls apart on basic accounting. I advocate replacing existing short-term Treasury debt, composed of bills and short-dated notes, with fixed-value floating-rate debt. The total amount of government debt in private hands need not change, so the total amount invested in the banking system and private credit markets need not change. An expansion of government debt overall can crowd out private lending, yes, but the form of government debt is of little consequence.

Fixed-Coupon Perpetuities

The United States should introduce perpetual long-term debt. This debt pays a \$1 coupon per bond, forever. As interest rates rise and fall, the price of perpetual debt will fall and rise. The Treasury will auction the debt at whatever price the market will pay. If (hopefully, when) an era of primary surpluses returns, the Treasury will repurchase outstanding debt at auction.

The Treasury can pay coupons of perpetual debt in shares of floating-rate debt, since the latter always carry the right to obtain reserves and therefore currency, and they can be used for tax payments. The Treasury can pay coupons daily, thus avoiding accrued-interest accounting.

Why?

As explained previously, perpetual debt folds all existing issues into one security, thus greatly deepening the market, liquidity, and collateral value of debt. Perpetual debt is the only way to produce a single security whose characteristic does not change with the passage of time. We should be rewarded with lower interest rates for the taxpayer as well as a better-functioning monetary and financial system.

For example, if the Treasury sells a thirty-year bond this year, that bond becomes a twenty-nine-year bond next year, when the Treasury sells a new thirty-year bond. These bonds are different securities. If their prices diverge,

Table 3-1. *Structure of U.S. Treasury Debt, March 2015*

Security	Number	Total value ($bn)[a]	Average issue size ($bn)
Bills	32	1,477	46
Notes	232	8,257	36
Bonds	67	1,608	24
TIPS	39	1,075	28
Floating	5	205	41
Total	375	12,621	

Source: Statement of the Public Debt (www.treasurydirect.gov/govt/reports/pd/mspd/2015/2015_mar.htm).

a. Numbers presented may not add up precisely to the totals due to rounding.

arbitrageurs cannot readily correct that difference. You cannot short-sell a thirty-year bond and deliver a twenty-nine-year bond in its place. If you hold the twenty-nine-year bond as collateral, you must deliver back a twenty-nine-year bond, not a thirty-year bond. If you want to buy a long-term bond, you have to choose either the twenty-nine or the thirty-year, and only half of the bondholders can bid on your offer.

And there are hundreds of different Treasury securities outstanding. My table 3-1 shows that the nearly $13 trillion of public debt is carved up in to 375 distinct securities, with typical issue sizes well below $50 billion each.

By contrast, if long-term debt were structured as a perpetuity, long-term debt would consist of a single issue, with trillions of dollars outstanding. New debt would be an expanded issue of the same security, literally the same CUSIP security identifier, completely fungible with outstanding debt. An investor buying or selling debt would face a market thousands of billions deep, not a few tens of billions. The spread in yields between on-the-run (newly issued) and off-the-run (older) issues would disappear, as all securities would be on-the-run. Arbitrage spreads between bonds with different coupon levels (Pancost 2015) would disappear. Bid-ask spreads would likely tighten, and the price impact of trading large blocks likely evaporate.

Already, U.S. debt is valued for its liquidity and collateral value. (For example, see Duffie 1996, Gorton and Ordoñez 2013, and Krishnamurthy and Vissing-Jorgensen 2012.) Yet liquidity and collateral value are not as great as they could be, evidenced not only by the existence of spreads, but also by occasional trading glitches (see Potter 2015) and reports of "collateral shortage" of liquid on-the-run Treasuries.

Price Impact

One may worry that when the Treasury repurchases debt, it will drive bond prices up, thereby paying more than it would have by paying the principal values of maturing debt. On reflection, this is unlikely to be a substantial problem.

Purchases affect prices, or raise bid-ask spreads, when the buyer conveys information by the offer or when a large purchaser show up unexpectedly. Treasury purchases to repay debt as a consequence of budget surpluses will convey no information about interest rate movements. And the Treasury's purchases will be slow, predictable, and widely preannounced.

The Treasury already sells debt with little price impact by auction. Since 2000, the Treasury has successfully repurchased outstanding issues, even illiquid and off-the-run issues, with little price impact. And one should compare any remaining price impact to the fees currently paid to roll maturing debt.

Call Option

One might want to complicate the debt by adding a call option. For example, the Treasury can always repurchase $1 perpetuities for $100. I do not think such a provision is desirable. The Treasury has abandoned the once-widespread inclusion of call options in existing long-term debt. The wisdom of that decision extends to perpetuities.

A call option complicates bond pricing. There is no simple formula for the value of a callable perpetuity.

A call option either requires a stated policy for when the call will be exercised, or it adds speculation about when the government will exercise its option, and pressure to call or not, with billions of dollars on the line. Calling the entire stock of debt and reissuing debt with a different call option could also be a momentous and expensive operation.

To what end? If it is to avoid the price impact of repurchasing debt on the market, adding a call option in today's liquid markets seems like a minor savings and a major headache. If it is to manage interest rate risk, it comes at the wrong time. Times when interest rates are low and bond prices are high are good times for government finance. If risk management is the goal, the Treasury should buy put options, the right to *sell* debt when rates are *high*.

In any case it would be better for the Treasury to buy call options directly. There is no reason in a modern financial market for the Treasury to bundle the bond with the call option.

Coupon Bonds and History

An obvious objection: since so much corporate and government debt consists of coupon bonds with principal payments at a finite maturity, surely there is a strong economic reason for this structure? I am not able to find one.

Government perpetuities are not a new idea. Some of the first government debt consisted of annuities and perpetuities. The towns of Douai and Calais sold annuities and perpetuities in 1260 (Kohn 1999, 5). Venice's 1262 *Monte* issued perpetual debt paying 5 percent interest semiannually.

Venice's debt, and that of other *Monti* such as Florence's, were also fully transferable, and publicly traded, in markets facilitated by brokers. Bonds were recorded in book-entry form and could be "encumbered with a lien as security for loans, for real estate transactions (to protect against defects of title), and for dowries. Indeed, shares were preferred to other forms of security because no litigation was necessary in case of default" (Kohn 1999, 10). The value of government debt as collateral goes back a long way, too!

More recently, perpetuities were the nearly exclusive source of financing for nineteenth-century Britain, including a 250 percent debt-to-GDP ratio at the end of the Napoleonic wars. Some early American debt was also issued without fixed maturity, starting with Alexander Hamilton's refunding of the 1790s (Homer and Sylla 1996, 189ff., 293).

Many early perpetuities had what we now call a call option—for example, being described as 3 percent perpetuities when the government had the right to repurchase each £3 of coupons for £100. However, in my reading, these options had a different purpose than the modern concept of an interest rate derivative. They allowed the government to pay back the debt when the government had the resources to do so, putting off repayment or roll-over in case of war or other time of fiscal stress, and they helped to overcome what might have been significant price impact of repurchases in an era of horse and sail communication. Yes, the option was used on occasion to lower coupons, as in "Goschen's conversion" of 1860 (Harley 1976)—which caused a lot of volatility, in line with my criticism—and the 2014 repurchase of 4 percent perpetual bonds issued in the 1920s (Stubbington and Edwards

2014). But the fact that governments occasionally use the interest rate option ex-post as an interest rate derivative does not imply that this option was centrally important for issuing the debt ex-ante.

Corporate bonds almost always have finite maturity and principal payments. Corporate perpetuities exist though they are rare. (ING sells perpetual exchange-traded debt with ticker INZ.)

There are several legal and accounting reasons why corporations might want to issue, and their investors demand, finite-maturity coupon plus principal debt.

In default, corporate bondholders are paid in proportion to the undiscounted principal amount of the bonds. This fact explains why investors demand a security with a stated principal value and sufficient coupons to bring the market value near par. The IRS may refuse to count perpetuities as debt for the deductibility of corporate taxes, and accounting or banking regulation may not count such perpetuities as a safe debt asset. Bankruptcy courts may put perpetual debt below other long-term unsecured debt. But none of these bankruptcy or tax issues apply to U.S. federal debt.

Default is not entirely unimportant. The United States has defaulted, for example, in the abrogation of gold clauses. The recent debt limit controversy raised the possibility of a technical if not economically important default, in the form of delayed coupon payments. A legal statement of rights in default will be an important part of perpetuity design. An otherwise meaningless par value, say, $20 for each $1 of coupon, is one possibility.

Corporate debt-holders might wish their debt to correspond to tangible assets or investment projects, and corporations typically do not have infinitely lived tangible assets against which to borrow. But U.S. federal debt is backed by the stream of net surpluses that the U.S. government can extract from taxpayers, which is a much longer-lived asset.

U.S. mortgages and mortgage-backed securities consist of a stream of coupons but no principal. This fact verifies that principal payments are not crucial for debt to be sold. The existence of the underlying asset (house) that can be seized on default adds to the suggestion that corporate principal is there to establish a claim in default.

In summary, I do not see in theory or experience an indication that there is something deeply wrong with perpetual government debt, especially for a solvent modern government of an advanced country borrowing its own currency.

Wholesale, Retail, and Hedging

Fixed-income markets demand a great variety of additional securities. People and institutions want to match specific liability streams, to hedge specific fixed-income risks, or to take other risks in pursuit of greater returns.

As a general vision, it seems best for the government to provide a few simple, deep, liquid, and default-remote benchmark securities, the provision of which is the government's unique comparative advantage. It is better for financial intermediaries to create products that fill the many varied and shifting specialized needs of retail individual, financial, and corporate clients, including coupon and zero-coupon bonds, mortgages and loans, customized swaps, caps, floors and other derivatives, annuities, life insurance, pension products, and estate planning products. And any fragmentation of Treasury debt lowers its depth and liquidity.

Treasury securities serve central price-discovery, hedging, and benchmarking functions. Several commenters have suggested that the Treasury should continue to offer a spectrum of coupon bonds, notes, and bills so that intermediaries can better price and hedge corporate bonds. On examination, however, I think this is a weak argument.

First, the STRIPs program can and should continue, by which coupon bonds are unbundled into zero-coupon elements.[3] Intermediaries will then have access to a deep and liquid market for zero-coupon debt, from which they can synthesize and price coupon bonds if they so desire. Strips based on perpetuities should be more abundant and more liquid than those based on current coupon bonds, since the distinction between principal and coupon strips will vanish and there is only one security to reconstitute.

---

3. A zero-coupon bond is a simple promise to pay $1 at a fixed point in time. A coupon bond is a bundle of zero-coupon bonds. STRIPS stands for the Treasury program "Separate Trading of Registered Interest and Principal of Securities," though "strip" is also the colloquial term for a zero-coupon bond formed from the pieces of a coupon bond. A quick view of the mechanics: "Under the STRIPS program, U.S. government issues with maturities of ten years or more became eligible for transfer over Fedwire. The process involves wiring Treasury notes and bonds to the Federal Reserve Bank of New York and receiving separated components in return. This practice also reduced the legal and insurance costs customarily associated with the process of stripping a security" (www.ny.frb.org/aboutthefed/fedpoint /fed42.html).

We do not need to create an infinite number of zeros. A perpetuity can be stripped, for example, into thirty annual zero-coupon bonds and a thirty-year futures contract.

I suggested that coupons be paid daily, to avoid accrued-interest accounting in bond sales and pricing. Zero-coupon strips issued at annual or quarterly intervals can then include accrued coupons, brought forward at the floating rate. The zero-coupon bond for December 31, 2025, for example, will be the cumulated value of $1 invested in floating-rate debt from January 1 to December 31 of 2025.

Second, with the advent of computers and modern fixed-income modeling, financial intermediaries do not need to observe comparable Treasuries in order to price and hedge corporate and other retail offerings. Almost all movements in the Treasury yield curve can be spanned with level, slope, and curvature factors, plus smaller liquidity, credit, and other factors. Today, fixed-income instruments are priced and hedged with liquid securities that span these factors, not with potentially illiquid Treasury instruments that replicate cash flows.

Third, corporate and municipal bonds are subject to credit risk and are typically callable. Valuing or hedging a corporate bond is not as simple as looking up a Treasury with similar coupon and maturity. Credit and liquidity spreads are fairly high-tech issues these days.

Fourth, valuing and hedging fixed-income securities, including call options, prepayment options, state-contingent default, and so forth, also requires one to measure, model, and hedge interest rate volatility. Volatility is poorly spanned by any combination of discount bonds.

Intermediate-Maturity Supply?

The question, then, is not whether an adequate number of liquid hedging instruments will exist. They will. If someone wants to buy a risk-free coupon bond, they will be able to do so. The question is whether markets inexorably demand to hold overall, netting out buyers and sellers, a character of securities different from what the Treasury can supply by a combination of fixed-value and fixed-coupon perpetuities and swaps between these two. Will an important scarcity premium emerge in the intermediate-maturity strip market?

To ponder this question, we must think about what characteristics of debt truly matter. Modern financial analysis recognizes the strong common movement among Treasury securities. We do not think of separate demands for, say, nine- and ten-year bonds, since they are such close substitutes. Instead, we start by recognizing that almost all movements in the yield curve (the plot of yield versus duration) correspond to level, slope, or curvature patterns. Then, the risk of any portfolio of Treasury securities is very well described by its duration and convexity—first and second derivatives of a bond's value with respect to its yield—or by its exposure to factors.

Now, by varying the supply of fixed-value and fixed-coupon debt, plus swaps between their cash flows, the Treasury can provide the market any duration it wants, any exposure to level versus slope shocks, and any special liquidity demand for fixed-value or fixed-coupon debt. Thus, a scarcity premium must mean that the market demands more or less overall exposure to the curvature factor (intermediate yields rise, long and short yields decline) or more or less convexity than the Treasury can provide after meeting the market's demand for duration or level and slope exposure.

Is that the case? Would such a demand, unmet, lead to a yield curve distortion significant enough to affect overall Treasury financing costs or the functioning of the financial system? We don't really know. But if it turns out to be the case, that doesn't mean we must keep 375 distinct coupon bonds and roll over half the debt each year. A single or small set of securities focused on providing the net exposure to curvature or convexity would do.

The Treasury could issue additional zero-coupon bonds. For example, the Treasury could issue ten-year zeros and let them mature, rolling over each matured issue to a new issue. The Fed could also issue strips in the middle of the term structure and buy long- and short-dated maturities.

Alternatively, the Treasury could issue a single additional perpetuity with a geometrically declining coupon.[4] For example, the coupon could be $1 in 2020 and decline 5 percent per year, paying $0.95 in 2021, $0.95^2 = $0.9025 in 2022, and so on. When the coupons get too small (say, $0.10), they can be re-based to $1 for convenience. This security behaves like an intermediate maturity bond. Yet it is always the same security through time, never needs to be rolled over, and allows the kind of market depth that the level perpetuity offers.

---

4. I thank John Campbell for this clever idea.

To be specific, the duration D of any bond measures how much a bond's price P falls when its yield y rises,

$$D = -\frac{1}{P}\frac{dP}{dy} = \frac{1}{y+g}.$$

For zero-coupon bonds, the duration equals the maturity. For a perpetuity whose coupons decline at rate g ($g=0$ for the level perpetuity), the duration is the inverse of $y+g$. So, at a 5 percent yield, the duration of the perpetuity is 20; it acts like a twenty-year zero-coupon bond. A perpetuity with a 5 percent declining coupon acts like a ten-year zero-coupon bond. This declining perpetuity also has less convexity than the level perpetuity and when stripped produces more short-dated zeros than long-dated zeros.

Darrell Duffie's thoughtful comment goes beyond demand for curvature or convexity to think about demand for specific issues. He notes, for example, occasional strong demand for the most recently issued ten-year coupon bond, driving its yield below those of very similar bonds, and episodes of collateral shortage and trading glitches for specific issues. He concludes that the Treasury must continue to issue two-, five-, and ten-year par-value nominal coupon bonds and carefully manage their supplies.

This is an important comment, eloquently summarizing objections I have heard from several financial market participants. It's especially important because these are precisely the kinds of problems that perpetuities are meant to solve by creating a single, very deep market.

The question is, whether an inexorable time-varying total demand for two-, five-, and ten-year par-value coupon bonds is written into the structure of the financial system? Or has supply created its own demand a benchmark effect typical of government debt markets? If the Treasury were to issue only a perpetuity, would we see collateral and hedging uses migrate to that new security, leaving behind a calm term structure of zeros? Or would my liquidity provision project fail, and we see large fluctuations in the price of synthetic two-, five-, and ten-year coupon bonds because of an unaltered underlying and fluctuating demand for those specific securities?

This is the core disagreement, and it is resolvable by data and experience. The Treasury can issue perpetuities together with the current spectrum of bonds, and the Treasury can wait to stop issuing current bonds until market demand has waned.

Accounting: Maturity and Face Value

One reason that current floaters have a two-year maturity is the question of how to account for their maturity. Perpetuities have infinite maturity, which would cause trouble with the Treasury's average maturity reports.

Maturity of coupon debt, variable-coupon debt, floating-rate debt, or debt with call or other options is a fairly meaningless concept. Weighted average maturity is a misleading guide to the Treasury's interest rate exposure, the frequency of rollovers, or much of anything else. Duration, convexity, three-factor sensitivities, and schedules of coupon and principal payments are better measures and easy to compute.

Much of the Treasury's accounting, including the *Treasury Bulletin* and Monthly Statements of the Public Debt, and the delightful "Debt to the Penny" website, report face values. Perpetuities have no meaningful face values. The Treasury will have to report the coupon value, market values, or use a benchmark yield.

These accounting and reporting issues should not get in the way of issuing useful securities. It's time to modernize the accounting, not to structure the debt around traditional but misleading numbers.

Tax-Free Debt

Treasury debt should be free of all tax, including personal and corporate income tax, capital gains tax, and estate taxes. The state and local exemption for federal interest should be extended to estate taxes and capital gains taxation. Strips created from tax-free debt should enjoy the same tax-free status.

Why?

Optimal taxation principles say not to tax rates of return, which discourages savings.[5] Perhaps reflecting these ideas, the U.S. government maintains a complex system of tax-sheltered investment vehicles. Tax-free federal debt would be a far simpler security to provide for some of the same purposes.

---

5. Judd (1985); Chamley (1986). See Atkeson, Chari, and Kehoe (1999) and Mankiw, Weinzierl, and Yagan (2009) for excellent reviews.

Borrowing and then taxing the interest is a curious practice. If the government taxes interest, people are willing to pay less for the debt up front. The government does not, in the end, borrow money on any better terms. An explicit analysis of this point follows.

Taxing capital gains of Treasury debt is a particularly curious practice. Bond prices are stationary, unlike stock prices. If bond prices fall this year, they must rise eventually. Thus, a capital gain this year must be matched by a capital loss in the future. Taxing realized capital gains makes Treasuries less liquid for taxable investors and thus for the market. We see complex capital-gains tax-avoidance strategies involving municipal debt, even though its interest is not taxable.

A substantial proportion of the taxation of Treasury debt is taxation of nominal interest that reflects inflation. Taxing inflationary gains is a bad idea.

The current market for Treasury debt is segmented, with few taxable investors holding any debt. Eliminating the taxation of federal debt will draw taxable investors back to the market, broadening demand for the debt.

In sum, by marketing what should be a very popular and liquid security, the government could sell more debt at lower net interest costs and improve economic efficiency.

The main motivation for taxing government debt is the idea that by doing so the Treasury avoids an implicit subsidy to high-tax-rate investors and thus pays less net interest overall. I demonstrate that this objection is very likely untrue. Offering the debt in tax-free form is likely to reduce the government's interest costs, save the economy substantial costs of tax evasion and sheltering, and reduce an implicit subsidy to nonprofit, well-sheltered, and foreign (nontaxed) investors. The basic reason is simple: high-tax-rate investors escape taxation by refusing to buy taxable Treasury debt in the first place. Maintaining high tax rates on income from Treasury securities only provides the illusion of progressive taxation.

It would be better for tax-free debt to be so defined, legally, and interest and capital gains not even declarable, rather than to offer tax exemptions for income from federal debt. The latter approach will be tempting, as it will allow Congress to maintain the appearance of progressive taxation and to limit the tax deductibility in various ways, likely excluding high-income households or other unpopular taxpayers, such as hedge funds or their managers with carried interest income, as it limits participation in other investment shelters. Congress would also be likely to include Treasury debt in an overall limit on deductions. The myRA program is essentially this complex structure.

But that approach would not make anything simpler. It would be much less likely to attract the high-tax and well-sheltered clientele back to Treasury debt. Most of all, deductibility provisions in the tax code can always be revisited. That may be good for an annual renegotiation between legislators, lobbyists, and beneficiaries. But it is not good for initial investment and raising the initial price of Treasury debt—the whole point of any savings.

Taxation of Treasury Debt

Treasury debt is subject to complex taxation of interest, capital gains, and in estates. Bonds issued at discount generate annual tax liabilities. Bonds purchased at premium generate a loss, which must be amortized against ordinary income. The inflation adjustments in TIPS generate taxable income.

There are some precedents for tax-free and tax-advantaged Treasury debt. Until 1942, many Treasury issues were fully tax exempt and traded at substantially higher prices (see Coleman, Ibbotson, and Fisher 1994, 26–27). Treasury debt is exempt from state and local income taxes. Federal taxes on savings bonds can be deferred until bonds are redeemed or reach final maturity, and interest can be excluded from tax altogether if the bondholder pays college tuition in the year that bonds mature or are sold.[6] Historically, some debt could be used at par to pay taxes, even if its current value was below par. In the myRA program, people can start a Roth IRA with Treasury investments. This is functionally tax-exempt Treasury debt, though with a lot of complex rules and income limits attached.

Returns on Treasury debt can also be sheltered. Yet sheltering any investment is a complex process. Put as much as possible into 401(k), 403(b), IRA, Roth IRA, and 526 accounts. Carefully time capital gains and losses. Mitt Romney's $100 million IRA based on capital gains of carried interest is a famous example. Plan estates carefully, setting up trusts early, gifting properly, arranging capital gains to occur post-gift, and so forth. Taxation can also be avoided by putting Treasury investments through tax-preferred intermediaries, such as pension funds, especially in the case of government or nonprofit employees, or life insurance.

IRA and similar plans may appear to tax rates of return, since they are taxed as ordinary income on withdrawal. But they do not. If you earn income Y, pay income taxes τY leaving after-tax income $(1 - \tau)Y$, and then are able to

---

6. See the U.S. Treasury website under "education planning" (www.treasurydirect .gov/indiv/planning/plan_education.htm).

invest with a tax-free return $(1+r)$, you end up with $(1-\tau)(1+r)Y$. If you earn income Y, invest the pretax earnings in an IRA that allows a tax-free return $(1+r)$, you have $(1+r)Y$ in your retirement account. You pay income taxes on withdrawal, leaving $(1-\tau)(1+r)Y$: exactly the same amount.

In sum, the Treasury already collects well below the statutory rates of taxation on Treasury interest, yet at a large cost in money and in simplicity. To a taxable investor, "buy it once and forget about all that" has great appeal.

Estate taxes are particular objects of costly avoidance. There's nothing like a once-per-generation 40 percent marginal rate, or the larger generation-skipping rate, to focus one's attention on estate planning and avoidance. As a result the Treasury gets little revenue from the estate tax and people spend a lot of money avoiding it. If Treasury debt were to pass unhindered through estates, that would truly bring back high-tax investors. If the Treasury can, as I suggest below, harvest current tax-avoidance costs, that would be a proportionally large amount.

Analysis of Tax-Free Debt

Here I verify analytically the claims I made above: First, the Treasury need not pay higher interest costs by issuing tax-free debt, because investors will pay more for that debt up front. Second, by offering tax-free debt the Treasury can harvest tax-avoidance costs and thereby lower its net interest costs. Third, when debt-holders pay different tax rates, the Treasury is likely to lower net interest costs, attract high-tax investors back to Treasuries, and eliminate a subsidy to nontaxed investors by offering tax-free debt.

Tax-Free Debt Need Not Raise Interest Costs

A simple example: Suppose the Treasury offers to pay a $10 coupon and $100 principal in a year, but taxes the coupon interest 50 percent. On net, the Treasury pays $5. If investors discount the future at 5 percent, they will offer $105/1.05 = $100 for the bond, and the Treasury pays net interest of 5 percent to borrow money. Now suppose that the Treasury offers the same $10 coupon tax-free. You might think that the Treasury now pays 10 percent to borrow money, but that would be wrong. Investors would be willing to pay more, $110/1.05 = $104.76, for the tax-free bond. And the Treasury pays the same 5 percent net interest to borrow money.

A bit more carefully, in the context of perpetuities, an investor facing tax rate τ will pay a price

$$P = \int_{t=0}^{\infty} e^{-rt}(1-\tau)1\, dt = \frac{1-\tau}{r}$$

for a taxable perpetuity, where r represents the discount rate for after-tax cash flows. To raise \$1, the Treasury must sell $B = 1/P = r/(1-\tau)$ bonds. Then, net of taxes, the Treasury pays interest $B(1-\tau) = r$ per period. The Treasury pays r in net interest to borrow \$1, no matter what tax rate is applied to Treasury interest.

This example emphasizes important but frequently overlooked principles of taxation. Taxing income or dividend streams is not the same thing as taxing rates of return. If the government taxes incomes or streams, prices change, potentially leaving rates of return unaffected. For example, corporate profits taxes are unlikely to be borne by shareholders. After a one-time capital loss when the tax is announced, lower stock prices offset higher corporate tax payments, leaving an unchanged rate of return.

Equivalently, the burden of taxation depends on the slope of supply and demand curves—that is, people's ability to change behavior to avoid taxes. In this simple example I assume a flat supply of capital at the after-tax rate of return r. Flat supply curves mean that suppliers do not bear any burden of taxation. I examine the flat supply curve assumption below. In a global capital market, replete with tax shelters for investments, it's a good place to start.

Raising taxes on interest would benefit the government *after* bonds have been sold. But once burned, twice shy investors will not offer the same price the next time around. I consider here only steady-state, long-run taxation in which prices fully reflect following payments, not the classic temptation for a just-this-once capital levy.

Tax-Avoidance Costs

By offering tax-free debt, the Treasury can collect the costs of tax avoidance and therefore lower interest costs overall.

Continue the simple example: the Treasury offers a one-year bond with \$100 principal, a \$10 taxable coupon, and 50 percent tax rate. Now, suppose that investors can pay \$1 to lawyers in order to cut the tax rate to 30 percent. The Treasury gets \$3, the lawyers get \$1, and the investor gets \$6. The investor is willing to pay \$106/1.05 = \$100.95 for the taxable bond and gets a 5 percent return. The Treasury, however, pays \$7 of net interest, so the Treasury pays an effective rate of $100 \times (107/100.95 - 1) = 5.99\%$. The Treasury has paid the tax-avoidance costs! The Treasury would do better by offering tax-free debt on which it pays only 5 percent as above.

In the context of the perpetuities, let the statutory tax rate be τ, let the proportional costs of tax avoidance be c, and let tax revenue received by the government be ρ, each per $1 of coupons. We have $\rho + c < \tau$, so tax avoidance is worthwhile to the investor. The government pays $1 in coupons and receives ρ back in taxes, so pays net interest $(1 - \rho)$ on each taxable bond. The investor receives a coupon of $1 and pays taxes ρ and avoidance costs c, so receives net coupon $(1 - \rho - c)$. A stream of taxable coupons is then worth $P = (1 - \rho - c)/r$ to the investor. Per $1 = P \times B$ borrowed by selling B bonds, then, the Treasury pays net interest

$$(1-\rho)B = \frac{1-\rho}{P} = \frac{1-\rho}{1-\rho-c}r > r.$$

By offering tax-free debt, Treasury pays only r, as above. By taxing interest, the Treasury ends up bearing the burden of tax-avoidance costs and raising its cost of funds.

Heterogeneous Tax Rates, Tax Clienteles, and Tax Efficiency

Different people pay different tax rates. If taxable and tax-free bonds give the same after-tax return at a tax rate τ^*, then it seems that tax-free debt is a present to investors who face higher tax rates. More generally, tax-free debt may be viewed as a loophole, the sort of thing that should be eliminated in a quest to broaden the base and lower overall tax rates.

By the same logic, however, this situation offers a subsidy to low-tax and nontaxed investors, including endowments, central banks, governments, non-profit corporations, many pension funds, and so forth. They receive an interest rate set by a marginal taxable investor who pays τ^*, yet they pay no tax. One could equivalently speculate that by offering nontaxable debt to everyone, these tax-exempt investors would receive the nontaxable rate like everyone else and the government would save interest costs.

The central issue is, who holds the debt and at what price they offer changes when the Treasury alters the tax treatment of debt. Whether interest costs rise or fall by offering nontaxable debt depends, among other things, on the supply curve—that is, on the availability of alternative investments. If all investors have access to alternatives with the same after-tax return r, then tax-free debt gives the lowest interest cost to the government. When capital can move, the Treasury can give some taxpayers presents but it cannot force taxpayers to suffer low returns.

Example in which Tax-Free Debt Lowers Interest Costs

Here is a simple calculation, following Miller's (1977) and Dybvig and Ross's (1986) tax-clientele models, in which offering tax-free debt lowers the Treasury's net interest costs.

Suppose that people facing tax rate τ demand up to X_τ dollars of debt, and thus $B_\tau = X_\tau/P$ bonds, as long as they can earn an after-tax return r. They are willing to pay up to $P = (1 - \tau)/r$ for each taxable perpetuity.

The government sells X dollars of taxable debt in a uniform-price auction. A price above $1/r$ attracts no buyers. A price of $P = 1/r$ attracts the tax-free investors, giving total demand of $X^d = X_0$. Lower prices then sweep out the demands of investors who face higher and higher tax rates. Supply equals demand $X = \int_0^{\tau^*} X_\tau \, d\tau$ then determines the cutoff tax rate τ^* and price $P = (1 - \tau^*)/r$.

Investors facing rate $\tau < \tau^*$ buy $B_\tau = X_\tau/P^* = X_\tau r/(1 - \tau^*)$ bonds. The government pays them net coupons

$$(1 - \tau)B_\tau = r\frac{1 - \tau}{1 - \tau^*} X_\tau,$$

so net coupons per dollar borrowed from these investors are

$$r\frac{1 - \tau}{1 - \tau^*} > r.$$

Investors facing tax rates $\tau > \tau^*$ don't buy any bonds.

Thus, all participating investors get a rate of return greater than or equal to their outside alternative, r. In this sense, taxable government debt is a subsidy to low-tax-rate investors.

The Treasury's total interest cost is the weighted average of what each investor gets,

$$r\int_0^{\tau^*} \frac{1 - \tau}{1 - \tau^*} \frac{X_\tau}{X} d\tau > r.$$

The Treasury pays more than r to finance the debt.

This model is consistent with observations of a downward-sloping demand curve for government debt, such as Krishnamurthy and Vissing-Jorgensen (2012), but by sweeping out marginal tax rates as debt must be sold to higher and higher tax clienteles, not from liquidity, segmented markets, preferred habitat, or signaling future monetary policy. This model also says that the yield ratio between government and municipal bonds should be related to the tax rate τ^* of the marginal investor for government bonds, not the maximum federal marginal rate. Thus the "muni bond puzzle"—that this interest spread is often lower than the maximum federal tax rate—is not necessarily a puzzle.

Now let the Treasury split its supply X into taxable X^T and nontaxable X^{NT} issues. The low-tax clientele will buy the taxable issues. But by offering a lower amount of these issues, the Treasury will not have to sweep so deeply into the high-tax rates, and it will pay a lower net rate on these issues. High-tax investors buy the tax-free debt. The Treasury pays a return r on the tax-free issues, also less than the net interest costs on all the previous issues. So total net interest costs decline.

To see how this works, let τ^* denote the new, lower tax rate of the marginal investor who buys taxable debt, determined now by $X^T = \int_0^{\tau^*} X_\tau \, d\tau$. Investors with tax rate $\tau > \tau^*$ now buy the nontaxable debt. They offer a price $P=1/r$ and buy what the government offers at that price. The Treasury's total interest payments are now the sum of taxable and nontaxable payments,

$$r \int_0^{\tau^*} \frac{1-\tau}{1-\tau^*} \frac{X_\tau}{X} d\tau + r \frac{X^{NT}}{X}.$$

Since τ^* has declined, overall the Treasury pays less by offering tax-free debt than it did by offering only taxable debt.

This model is admittedly stylized. Still, it captures important real-world considerations: (1) Selling debt at taxable rates to nontaxed or less-taxed investors implies a subsidized rate of return. Selling nontaxed debt to all investors removes that subsidy. (2) The idea that the government does better by taxing the yields of high-rate investors relies on the belief that such investors will buy government debt despite suffering rates of return lower than they can get elsewhere.

Example in which Taxable Debt Lowers Interest Costs

With a model in hand, one can spot the central assumption: that all investors have access to the same after-tax alternative opportunity r. One might say "yes, municipal bonds," but another might swiftly answer that the government should get rid of the municipal bond exemption.

Here is the opposite possibility. Suppose each investor facing tax rate τ has a best alternative investment that yields an after-tax rate of return $(1-\tau)r$. All of the investor's investment possibilities are fully taxed, at the same rate. Now each investor is willing to pay the same price

$$P = \int_{t=0}^{\infty} e^{-(1-\tau)rt}(1-\tau)\,dt = \frac{1}{r}$$

for taxable perpetuities. Each investor is willing to pay even more

$$P = \int_{t=0}^{\infty} e^{-(1-\tau)rt}\,dt = \frac{1}{(1-\tau)}\frac{1}{r}$$

for tax-free perpetuities.

If the Treasury issues only taxable perpetuities in this case, who buys them is indeterminate as each investor is indifferent. Let $\hat{X}_\tau \le X_\tau$ denote the dollar value of debt actually bought by investors facing tax rate τ, with $\int_{\tau=0}^{1}\hat{X}_\tau\,d\tau = X =$ supply. The Treasury then pays overall net interest

$$r\int_{\tau=0}^{1}(1-\tau)\frac{\hat{X}_\tau}{X}\,d\tau. \tag{3-1}$$

The Treasury does better if debt happens to be in the hands of highest tax rate investors.

If the Treasury instead issues a mix of taxable and nontaxable debt, then the high-tax investors will buy the nontaxable debt. We will sweep out a similar demand curve for *nontaxable* debt starting at the *highest* tax rates. The cutoff tax rate τ^* and corresponding price $P = 1/[(1-\tau^*)r]$ will be set by supply = demand for nontaxable debt $X^{NT} = \int_{\tau^*}^{1} X_\tau\,d\tau$. Each high-tax-rate investor buys bonds $B_\tau = X_\tau/P = X_\tau(1-\tau^*)r$, each of which pays a net coupon of \$1.

The Treasury's overall net interest cost is now the sum of what it pays to low-tax investors and to high-tax investors,

$$r\int_{\tau=0}^{\tau^*}\frac{(1-\tau)\hat{X}_\tau}{X}\,d\tau + \int_{\tau^*}^{1}\frac{(1-\tau^*)X_\tau}{X}\,d\tau. \tag{3-2}$$

The overall rate, in equation (3-2), could be either higher or lower than it is with all taxable debt in equation (3-1). It seems that interest costs go up, because the right-hand term replaces $(1-\tau)$ with $(1-\tau^*)$ in the region $\tau > \tau^*$ But the distribution of debt holdings $\hat{X}_\tau$ changes. If actual debt holdings were less than capacity $\hat{X}_\tau < X_\tau$ in this high-tax region of (3-1), then those investors will buy more debt $\hat{X}_\tau = X_\tau$ in (3-2). In that case, then debt holdings $\hat{X}_\tau$ must decline in the low-tax, first term of (3-2) and net interest costs decline.

Thus, if in equation (3-1) the taxable debt happened to be in the hands of high-tax-rate investors, so the left-hand term of (3-2) was already zero and quantities held do not change across tax rates, then replacing $1-\tau$ in (3-1) with $1-\tau^*$ in the right-hand term of (3-2) will raise the government's interest costs. This is the case for taxing debt. However, if in (3-1) the taxable debt happened to be in the hands of low-tax-rate investors so that $\hat{X}_\tau = 0$ for $\tau \geq \tau^*$, then the Treasury's interest costs will decline on the introduction of tax-free debt. The government will attract all the high-tax-rate investors to participate, shifting holdings from the left-hand term of (3-2) to its right-hand term.

In sum, introducing tax-free debt can raise the government's interest costs if (1) high-tax investors receive lower after-tax returns on all their alternative investment opportunities, and also (2) taxable government debt is already in the hands of high-tax investors.

Which View Is Right?

Miller (1977) argued that all investors can get the same after-tax alternative return r. One can hold stocks that pay most of their returns as capital gains and not realize capital gains, then step up the basis in estates. One can shield investments in tax-deferred strategies or in real estate, privately held businesses, and other nonmarket investments.

Few U.S. taxable investors hold long-term Treasury debt. *Treasury Bulletin* Table OFS-2, excerpted in my table 3-2, lists $17 trillion in debt. Of this amount, $7 trillion is held by government accounts, which pay no taxes, leaving $10 trillion held by the public, while $5.8 trillion—more than half—is held by foreigners. The Federal Reserve Foreign Portfolio Holdings[7] lists that

7. Foreign Portfolio Holdings of U.S. Securities as of June 30, 2013, table 12, Department of the Treasury, Federal Reserve Bank of New York, Board of Governors of the Federal Reserve System, April 2014 (www.treasury.gov/ticdata/Publish/shla 2013r.pdf).

almost all of the debt held by foreigners is $4.9 trillion "long-term" debt, of which $3.6 trillion is held by "foreign official" investors, largely central banks. Table FD-5 of the *Treasury Bulletin*[8] lists only $6.5 trillion debt greater than one year outstanding at the end of 2013, suggesting that less than $1.6 trillion long-term debt is held by any U.S. investor. The rising yield curve means that more taxable interest comes from longer-maturity debt, so the fact that long-maturity debt is so overwhelmingly held by foreign nontaxable investors further reduces taxes on interest.

Back to my table 3-2, $1.1 trillion is held by mutual funds. To the extent that those mutual funds are held by nonprofit or tax-exempt entities or in tax-exempt or deferred accounts, they escape taxation. Private pension funds are tax favored[9] if not tax exempt. State and local governments pay no taxes. Savings bond interest can be deferred or eliminated. The $1.2 trillion held by "other investors," represent a mix of tax rates and tax-avoidance strategies.

The Flow of Funds[10] gives a similar breakdown of $12,756 billion Treasury, agency, and federal mortgage debt held by the public, with households holding only $547 billion "bills and other Treasury securities." Corporate and noncorporate businesses hold a tiny $40 billion and $52 billion each, and the rest of the world holds $6 trillion.

In sum, the majority of Treasury debt is held by investors who are paying low or no tax rates on interest they receive.

How much revenue does the United States earn by taxing Treasury debt? This question should be answerable from IRS tax return data. I have not found a source that attempts this calculation. The answer is important.

Lowering interest costs is not the beginning and end of optimal taxation. And these models are very simplistic. But the intuition that offering tax-free debt will lower government revenues or subsidize high-income taxpayers is not in general correct, and quite plausibly incorrect.

---

8. U.S. Department of the Treasury, *Treasury Bulletin*, Table FD-5—Maturity Distribution and Average Length of Marketable Interest-Bearing Public Debt Held by Private Investors, p. 27 (www.fiscal.treasury.gov/fsreports/rpt/treasBulletin /current.htm).

9. Tax Policy Center, Joint Project of the Urban Institute and Brookings Institution (www.taxpolicycenter.org/taxtopics/encyclopedia/pensions.cfm).

10. Financial Accounts of the United States, Federal Reserve Statistical Release Z.1, June 11, 2015, table L.209, p. 99 (www.federalreserve.gov/releases/z1/current/z1 .pdf).

Table 3-2. *Ownership of Treasury Securities*

Ownership	$billions
Total public debt	17,352
SOMA and intragovernmental holdings	7,205
Total privately held	10,147
Depository institutions	321
U.S. savings bonds	179
Private pension funds	492
State and local government pension funds	203
Insurance companies	264
Mutual funds	1,121
State and local governments	593
Foreign and international	5,793
Other investors[a]	1,179

Sources: *Treasury Bulletin* Table OFS-2, values for December 2013; U.S. Department of the Treasury, *Treasury Bulletin*, Table FD-5—Maturity Distribution and Average Length of Marketable Interest-Bearing Public Debt Held by Private Investors, p. 27 (www.fiscal.treasury.gov/fsreports/rpt/treasBulletin/current.htm).

a. Includes individuals, government-sponsored enterprises, brokers and dealers, bank personal trusts and estates, corporate and noncorporate businesses, and other investors.

Indexed Debt

Indexed debt should be perpetual and pay a coupon equal to $1 times the current consumer price index (CPI). The March 2015 CPI is 236.119. Indexed debt would thus pay a coupon of $2.36119 for each bond, on an annualized basis. If the CPI rises to 250 in 2020, then indexed debt will pay a coupon of $2.50. If the CPI declines to 200, then indexed debt will pay a coupon of $2.

Why?

TIPS were a great start. But they can be improved. TIPS increase coupons and principal for inflation, but they do not decrease coupons if the CPI falls below its value on their issue date. As a result, TIPS include an inflation option. And new issues contain a different inflation option than old issues. TIPS have a complex tax treatment. Inflation adjustments to principal trigger immediate tax liabilities. Taxation of the inflation adjustment means that TIPS do not fully protect against inflation.

This heterogeneity and complex tax treatment hinders the collection of TIPS into tax-efficient mutual funds and muddies their use as inflation hedges. TIPS are, partially as a result, illiquid and not nearly as popular as economists expected.

In modern portfolio theory, a nontaxable indexed perpetuity is the central riskless asset for long-term investors (Campbell and Viceira 2001; Cochrane 2014a; Wachter 2003). If you invest in a tax-free indexed perpetuity, you can consume a steady amount forever and ignore mark-to-market price variation. By contrast, there really is no portfolio problem to which thirty years of coupons and a big principal payment are the answer.

Under the gold standard, Victorian perpetuities offered a real payment essentially immune from substantial inflation. At least there is a historical precedent for the popularity of such a security. Barro (1999) argues that indexed perpetuities are the optimal form of debt finance.

Indexed perpetuities should offer the Treasury lower-cost long-term financing than nominal perpetuities. Investors will accept lower interest rates in return for protection from inflation risk. As evidence of lower borrowing costs, the yield curve was downward sloping or flat in the nineteenth century, when the gold standard enforced long-run price stability. The Treasury's TIPS and the United Kingdom's inflation-indexed yield curves have also typically been flatter or more inverted than the corresponding nominal yield curves. A better security should enhance this phenomenon. Most economic interest rate models produce a downward sloping average real term structure. Since the indexed perpetuity is the riskless long-term asset, long-run investors demand compensation for the greater long-run reinvestment risk of short-term assets (Campbell, Shiller, and Viceira 2009).

In sum, as with all these innovations, offering a simple, liquid, and popular security should allow the Treasury to finance deficits at lower cost, as well as to improve the functioning of financial markets.

TIPS already serve an important monetary policy function: they allow the Federal Reserve to obtain a direct measure of market-based inflation expectations. However, the illiquidity and complex tax treatment of TIPS makes that tea-leaf reading more obscure than it needs to be. The spread between my indexed perpetuities and nominal perpetuities (or strips or swaps based on these securities) would provide a cleaner measure of expected inflation.

Objections and Extensions

An indexed perpetuity does not directly provide inflation protection for shorter-horizon returns. For example, suppose an investor wants to save for college tuition in ten years. That investor wants an inflation-indexed zero-coupon bond, not an indexed perpetuity.

Inflation-indexed perpetuities can and should be stripped just like nominal perpetuities. This stripping would yield a market in zero-coupon inflation-indexed bonds. These zero-coupon bonds are natural inflation hedges for discrete-horizon returns, and they can be assembled to be inflation hedges for other nominal fixed-income instruments. As with nominal perpetuities, it seems best for the Treasury to provide the simplest benchmark security and let private intermediaries create more specialized products.

The price index is a tricky issue. The CPI is imperfect. Improvements in its measurement will impact coupon payments. For example, the change from fixed to chain-weighted CPI was an improvement. The treatment of housing costs and quality changes will surely improve. The future will likely include more real-time data, following the example of the MIT Billion Prices Project.[11] Yet, as we have seen with Social Security, index improvements may be fought by those who will be paid less as a result.

Also, governments such as Argentina in serious inflation and with outstanding inflation-indexed debt have been known to meddle with the CPI calculation. Investors might worry about the same issue in the United States.

Do investors need some stronger legal rights regarding inflation adjustments? Current TIPS simply specify that the holder will be paid based on the CPI as calculated by the Labor Department. Bondholders seem content with the competence and independence of the Bureau of Labor Statistics (BLS). However, we don't have a lot of inflation and have not seen big changes in its computation. Since bondholders may sue the Treasury or BLS in the event of any big changes, establishing the form for such debate ahead of time is a worthy thought.

Beyond supply and liquidity effects, my view that inflation-indexed debt will result in lower cost does assume that inflation risk premiums are valued differently by the Treasury and investors, or that the Treasury expects lower inflation than investors expect. Throughout, I presume a sober and solvent U. S.

---

11. The Billion Prices Project aims to measure inflation quickly and precisely by scraping prices from the Internet. See http://bpp.mit.edu/usa/.

government that wishes to produce strong noninflationary growth. Like any capital levy, offering nonindexed debt and then inflating it away is cheaper. Once.

TIPS include an inflation option, that coupons and principal are not adjusted downward past the value on their date of issue. There is no economic reason for this option. Why should an investor who wants a steady inflation-protected stream desire, and pay for, a security that rises in real value in deflation? The option may have been added as a sweetener to better market the securities. But the option costs money and makes the security needlessly complex.

Variable-Coupon Debt

Long-term debt should include the right of the government to temporarily lower the coupon, without triggering legal default.

One can imagine all sorts of legal or implicit rules for raising and lowering coupons. On balance, I think the following structure will be most useful and suffer the least problems. The debt includes a promise—for example, a $1 coupon. But the government has the right to suspend or to lower those coupon payments temporarily. The coupon functions like interest payments of noncumulative preferred stock, not the coupons of regular debt—where missed coupons trigger default—or the dividends of regular equity—where dividends are freely variable.

The expectation that the government will restore coupons when the temporary exigency has passed will give the debt value during the reduction of coupons. It also allows the government to sell debt in the first place and even to sell additional debt during a coupon suspension.

This feature applies only to long-term debt. The government does not have the legal right to devalue fixed-value debt relative to reserves and currency.

Why?

Variable-coupon perpetuities would allow the Treasury to quickly manage temporary fiscal problems by lowering coupons, without triggering default or inducing inflation.

Both default and inflation incur far-reaching economic damage. A legal default means widespread lawsuits and attempts to seize assets or revenues or to refuse to pay taxes. Even a technical default, such as delayed coupon payments during a debt-ceiling fracas, could seize up the financial system. Imagine how much easier the Greek debt crisis would have been if Greece did not need to roll over any debt and had the legal authority to cut coupon payments for a while.

This option would be used sparingly. The height of the Civil War might have been one case, as an alternative to greenback inflation. World War II might have been financed with debt whose coupons would start at war's end. Other advanced countries, such as the United Kingdom in the two world wars, have experienced sufficient stress at times that this feature might have been appropriate.

This is not a provision wisely used for regular countercyclical policy. The United States can easily finance the vast majority of cyclical or even war-related deficits by borrowing more, while still paying coupons. This provision is crucial when credit markets may refuse those options.

As with other kinds of debt, the Treasury could test the waters by issuing some variable-coupon debt and then increasing the amount as markets get used to the idea. However, in this case, more is better. If one-tenth of the debt has variable coupons, then those coupons must be cut ten times as much to provide the same budget relief. Investors pricing the bonds will know this fact and charge a larger spread for a small issue. So the spreads of a small test-the-waters issue will not be a good measure of the spreads when most debt is variable-coupon. Furthermore, perpetuities don't naturally mature. Converting perpetuities to variable-coupon status requires the Treasury to repurchase the old ones and issue new ones, which is an expensive proposition.

Rules, Reputations, and Temptations

There are many proposals for government debt with variable-coupon or principal repayment. The most common are bonds with repayment linked by formula to GDP. Borensztein and Mauro (2004) advocate debt with repayment linked to GDP growth. Kamstra and Shiller (2010) advocate "Trills," bonds whose repayment varies with the level of GDP. Miyajima (2006) offers a longer literature review, history, and pricing analysis. Geddie (2014) covers some recent experience with GDP-linked debt in Greece and Argentina, along with investor's doubts.

A rule can help to assure investors and commit the government not to needlessly or perpetually lower coupons. Violation of the rule can trigger legal actions, asset seizures, or other formal sanctions in addition to a more visible loss of reputation.

Rules also have disadvantages. Coupons linked to GDP cannot be varied based on a war, a fiscal shock, a financial crisis, bankruptcy of states or their pensions, a sharp commodity-price or terms-of-trade shock, and so forth. GDP-linked debt would have specified a reduction in coupons in 2008–09 during a collapse of interest rates, a flight *to* U.S. debt, and the easiest money-borrowing period in memory for the Treasury, precisely the wrong time.

Some GDP-linked debt proposals are designed as a precommitment to countercyclical fiscal stimulus, more than devices to avoid unexpected fiscal stress. If that's a good idea, budget rules are just as easy.

One could write more rules to create a richly complex state-contingent debt, but it seems fairly pointless to try to do so. Corporations do not pay dividends mechanically linked to sales or profit numbers for just these reasons.

Yes, governments will be tempted to lower coupons ex-post. And there will be strong forces resisting that temptation or pressing for a restoration of coupons in a suspension. First, a large class of voters and otherwise politically influential owners of the debt act as the shareholders of a corporation do, demanding dividend payments and forcing a change of management if they are unhappy with dividends. From the founding of the Bank of England through Hamilton's assumption of Revolutionary War debt to the present, powerful bondholders help to have debts repaid or not inflated away. Second, any reduction in coupons that is not quickly or predictably reversed will damage the value of the debt and the government's ability to issue new debt. A desire to build up its creditworthiness and maintain the value of its debt will impel the government to pay coupons and to clearly explain why coupons are suspended and under what contingencies they will be restored.

The temptation to lower coupons is not qualitatively different from the temptation to inflate nominal debt, or the temptation to default explicitly. A government that can issue nominal debt and not inflate it away, that can issue foreign currency debt and not default, has already solved the first-order precommitment issues needed to issue variable-coupon debt and not immediately lower the coupons.

Coupons could be freely variable, like corporate dividends. But corporations have clearer structures for representing stockholder interests. Bondholders alone do not elect governments. Freely varying coupons, rather than a promise that is temporarily suspended, would also lead to continual political debate over the level of coupons.

Economics and History

A long history of economic literature studies the proper way for governments to handle fiscal and economic shocks.

The legal rights of large-country sovereign debt are weaker than those of private debt, since bondholders can't take over the government or place the country in bankruptcy. The huge sovereign debt literature studies the question of whether and to what extent reputations alone can substitute for legal and other costs of default. Bulow and Rogoff (1989) argue that reputation alone is not enough for small countries. Eaton and Fernandez (1995) and Aguiar and Amador (2014) are recent reviews. A superficial summary is that reputations may help, but additional precommitment mechanisms that help to induce repayment are valuable.

I have alluded to some of these mechanisms, including the political power of bondholders and the political costs of violating rules and traditions. In my view, these are sufficient to allow discretionary variable-coupon debt of the sort I have described to function, and for a government that is already able to precommit not to default or inflate standard kinds of debt. I do not think a legally binding rule linking payments to GDP or other indices is necessary—or worth the loss of flexible state-contingency and the costs of litigation over the index.

Lucas and Stokey (1983) present the classic analysis of optimal state-contingent debt payments. Governments could react to fiscal shocks by raising distorting taxes. State-contingent default allows more smoothing of such taxes and hence fewer economic distortions.

Lucas and Stokey's "default" can be interpreted as actual default, as inflation, or as my proposed reduction in coupon payments. The choice between distorting taxes, explicit default, inflation, or variable-coupon debt hinges on costs of the last three, which Lucas and Stokey do not consider.

Long-term debt is already a useful fiscal stabilizer (Cochrane 2001; Debortoli, Nunes, and Yared 2014). When bond investors see trouble ahead, the relative price of long-term debt can fall and give the government some time to solve its problem. If the government has issued only short-term debt, then either the price level must rise or the government faces a rollover crisis.

The fiscal theory of the price level (see Cochrane 2005 for an introduction and references) interprets inflation as a Lucas-Stokey state-contingent default. Shocks to inflation lower the real value of government debt. This adjustment on nominal debt is automatic, not needing government action, and avoids default costs. Nominal debt is like corporate equity. For these features, Sims (2001) argues for nominal debt rather than indexed or foreign-currency debt.

However, inflation is not costless either. Inflation engineers a transfer from private lenders to borrowers, and in the presence of price-stickiness drags down the macroeconomy as well. Schmitt-Grohé and Uribe (2004, 2005) argue that even with a small amount of price-stickiness, the reduction in distorting taxes produced by implicit state-contingent default via inflation is swamped by the macroeconomic damage of inflation. In their model, the government should react to fiscal shocks by relying more on distorting taxation than by default via inflation. Variable-coupon debt is even better: it allows a state-contingent default with no increase in distorting taxation, inflation, or explicit default costs.

High ex-post costs are, admittedly, useful ex-ante precommitments. Tying government default to painful inflation, harming private contracts and the macroeconomy, widens the group of voters who are opposed to inflation and implicit default and lowers its attractiveness to a government. On the other hand, a desirable government state-contingent default may coincide with desirable private state-contingent defaults. The latter view motivates some current advice for large inflation in the United States and Eurozone, to wash away the perceived "overhang" or "balance sheet drag" of large private as well as public debts.

The most salient danger of variable-coupon debt, then, is the same as its advantage. It reduces the costs of lowering coupons. A government fearful of the budgetary and economic consequences of formal default will work harder to avoid it. The threat of chaos was important to resolving the last debt-ceiling fracas. My suggested structure of a rare provision to be used in extremis is an attempt to put some significant costs in the way of coupon reductions.

This brief review takes us deep into the questions I avoid in this essay: how to *use* the tools I advocate; *when* and under what limitations to lower coupons. By quickly surveying this literature we see the point here: that variable-coupon debt, like the other securities I advocate, is a good tool. Governments need to then make the harder decisions about when to use the tools.

Historically, the United Kingdom suspended convertibility of currency and hence government debt into gold during wars. It then restored convertibility at par after the war. The expectation of this restoration buoyed the value of currency and debt during the war, and the restoration gave bondholders confidence to lend in advance and during the next war. This historical experience should give us some comfort that discretionary suspensions and restorations can work.

However, this policy led to some inflation during the war, followed by sometimes painful disinflation after the war, as in the 1920s. While similar in spirit, suspending coupons on long-term debt rather than suspending the convertibility of short-term debt should help to isolate government finances from inflation and these undesirable macroeconomic consequences.

Swaps

The Treasury should originate and trade swap contracts between these forms of debt. Swap contracts exchange cash flows without buying and selling bonds or exchanging any money up front. For example, a fixed-for-floating swap exchanges a fixed amount y per year in exchange for the floating rate paid to $1 of fixed-value debt. The quantity y is determined so that no money changes hands up front. Similarly, an inflation swap trades a fixed amount y per year for the $1 \times$ CPI paid by an indexed perpetuity. Here, I describe a very simple implementation of such swap contracts.

Why?

One of the Treasury's tasks is to manage the maturity structure of government debt. The Treasury balances, among other considerations, its sense of which debt offers the lowest long-run financing cost, the danger to the budget of rising interest rates, and the macroeconomic and financial effects of different maturity structures. Currently, the Treasury manages interest exposure and maturity structure primarily by changes in the maturity of newly offered debt. Repurchases are smaller and rarer.

Swap contracts would allow the Treasury to adjust the government's interest rate or inflation exposure quickly. A large fraction of Treasury securities lies in the proverbial sock drawers of long-term investors. Buying and selling a trillion dollars of debt would be difficult. Buying and selling a trillion dollars of swap contract exposure would be much simpler, as much less cash needs to be moved. This is why even small banks routinely adjust interest exposure via swaps rather than by buying and selling bonds, mortgages, deposits, and so forth.

Most of all, swap contracts will allow the Treasury to separate the liquidity provision, debt financing, and risk management functions of the debt. For example, the Treasury could meet a large, money-like demand for fixed-value floating-rate debt, but swap out the interest rate risk to the budget with a large fixed-for-floating swap. The money-like demand attaches to the security itself, not to the interest rate risk exposure, so the swap does not undo the benefits of the floating-rate issue.

Implementation

Since we will observe the price of fixed-coupon perpetuities in liquid markets, and since the value of floating-rate debt is always $1, pricing and reselling Treasury swap contracts can be easy. This fact allows for a simple structure of Treasury swap markets.

Denote the price of perpetuities at time t by P_t, and denote the floating rate r_t. The swap counterparty has a Treasury account with holdings of fixed-value floating-rate debt. For each $1 of notional swap value, the Treasury will pay (or receive) in each time interval Δ (e.g., $\Delta = 1/365$) an amount

$$(1 - P_t r_t)\Delta + (P_{t+\Delta} - P_t)$$

into the counterparty's holdings of fixed-value floating-rate debt.

How does this work? A swap that uses floating-rate debt as collateral, marked to market daily, is the same thing as financing the purchase of a fixed-coupon perpetuity at the floating rate. If the Treasury lends you P_t, and you use it to buy one perpetuity, then the next day you receive a coupon $1 \times \Delta$, you pay interest $P_t r_t \Delta$, and the value of your long-term bond increases or decreases by $(P_{t+\Delta} - P_t)$. These are exactly the payments specified by my swap contract.

If prices fall, the counterparty starts losing money. At some point, the counterparty will have to top up its holdings of floating-rate debt, which function as collateral to this swap contract. If the counterparty's holdings drop to zero and the counterparty does not post more floating-rate debt, the contract is canceled.

How is this contract different from a regular swap? The most important difference is the nature of collateral: fixed-value floating-rate debt (i.e., cash). A conventional swap contract would allow the counterparty to post other collateral, so if the counterparty didn't have a lot of (interest-paying) cash, the counterparty could pledge other securities instead.

In my view, the Treasury should not be in the business of taking, evaluating, seizing, and selling collateral. Parties wishing to post such collateral should use that collateral for a loan from a financial institution and then use the proceeds of the loan to increment their Treasury floating-rate holdings. Or, such a party should enter directly into the secondary swap market with financial institutions.

The remaining differences between this implementation and a standard swap contract enhance the simplicity and liquidity of this contract. If the Treasury were to enter regular swap contracts, then each contract would be different, based on a different initial value of the perpetuity. In this system, there is a single, resalable, instantly cancelable contract that is the same for everyone.

Counterparties

Who will buy swaps? First of all, the same banks, financial institutions, foreign central banks, insurers, pensions, and others that deal in and hold Treasury debt. The security that is ideal for the Treasury to manage interest rate risk is also ideal for these institutions to manage interest rate risk, or to take on interest rate risk for a price.

What if the counterparties fail? Swaps are collateralized, so despite the large payments involved, the Treasury's exposure to credit risk is nil. And the Treasury has certain advantages over other derivatives creditors in getting paid on the failure of financial institutions, especially the large dealer banks. Furthermore, the huge Dodd-Frank bureaucracy and the Fed's regulators and stress-testers charged with supervising the complex risks undertaken by financial institutions can surely monitor interest rate exposure in plain-vanilla Treasury swap transactions.

The market can be broader. Currently, swap transactions are only available to relatively large financial institutions. The very simple structure of Treasury swaps I describe could open up a retail market, as there is no reason for the Treasury to limit participation in these contracts at all. Homeowners concerned about the effect of interest rate increases on their mortgages, or small businesses worried about their rent and leases, could buy swaps on the Treasury website, just as they buy bills and savings bonds.

Concluding Comments

I introduce a set of tools, but I only touch on the vast literature recommending how to use these tools. Should the Treasury issue primarily short-term debt to harvest the term premium, or long-term debt to insure the Treasury and the price level against fiscal shocks? Greenwood, Hanson, Rudolph, and Summers argue for the former in chapter 1. I argue (Cochrane 2001) for the latter. (See also Faraglia and others 2014.) How much debt of each category should Treasury sell? Should the Treasury fix prices instead and let relative quantities follow market demands? How much inflation risk should the Treasury keep or transfer via indexed debt or swaps? Under what circumstances should the Treasury temporarily reduce coupon payments? How should it change debt quantities, prices, or relative prices in response to macroeconomic, financial, and fiscal events?

These questions span the modern literature on taxation, debt, fiscal and monetary policy, and financial structure. This literature does not yet provide widely accepted answers. But that is not a reason not to introduce the tools. We've had simple government debt for over 800 years, and we are still discussing its optimal use. Both sides of each debate would find improved tools useful. And having the tools in hand may spur better thought on how to use them.

Use of all of these tools, and conventional Treasury debt, has simultaneous repercussions for fiscal policy, for monetary policy as it is now broadly construed, for the macroeconomy, for inflation, and for financial market structure and stability. These concerns are currently spread out over many federal agencies and their constituencies. For example, the maturity question affects monetary and fiscal policy. While the Treasury has been issuing long-term debt to take advantage of low rates and to lock in low financing costs, the Federal Reserve has been buying up that debt and issuing short-term debt (reserves) in quantitative easing. In chapter 1, Greenwood, Hanson, Rudolph, and Summers point out this loggerhead and advocate a new Fed–Treasury accord over who is in charge of the maturity structure. Similarly, selling more indexed debt exposes the budget to more inflation risk, but may save financing costs and help to lower inflation. I advocate selling more floating-rate debt to engender more financial stability, a concern of the financial stability part of the Fed, the Securities and Exchange Commission (SEC), and other agencies. A larger coordination or "accord" will clearly be desirable.

I introduced fixed-value floating-rate, indexed and nominal fixed-coupon perpetuities, in taxable and tax-free form, and long-term debt that allows reductions in coupon payments. Not all these securities are necessary. I see no advantage of having both taxable and tax-free debt, so I recommend issuing all debt in tax-free form only. I recommend that all long-term debt contain the legal right to reduce coupon payments. This is a feature that would be used sparingly. But when it's needed, the more debt that can have coupons reduced, the better. I think the United States should issue both nominal and indexed debt, however, as that distinction will give better measurement and control of inflation. Nominal debt is also a useful buffer, and as corporations issue both debt and equity, so the government should issue both indexed and nominal debt.

In all cases except variable coupon, though, having both versions does little harm, other than to subdivide the debt into somewhat less deep and liquid versions. Likewise, all of these forms of debt can be introduced gradually, and current debt can slowly run off once experience confirms the value of the new forms of debt.

I advocate tools that allow the United States to borrow more and at lower interest rates. A strand of comment warns against this course. The debt is large and our government's ability to pay it off is in question. Innovations that make borrowing easier, in this view, are to be avoided. Similar "starve the beast" arguments have been made that the United States should not adopt a more efficient tax system. I note the argument, and hope that our democracy is strong enough to limit its borrowing, spending, and taxation voluntarily, and not by tying our government to deliberately inefficient tax and debt structures.

As I write in spring 2015, it is a benign moment for U.S. debt. Interest rates are at historic lows, interest rate volatility is low, and inflation is nearly nonexistent. U.S. government debt remains a safe haven. Few outside the regulatory agencies and academia are worrying about financial stability and how much it could be improved by the diffusion of fixed-value run-proof Treasury debt. Hedging inflation risk, hedging interest rate risk, and avoiding the taxation of Treasury interest are not high on the public agenda. These facts are unheralded benefits of a zero-rate, zero-inflation configuration. Planning for fiscal shocks in which the United States has trouble borrowing or rolling over debt is not high on many agendas, either.

But benign times may not last. The Federal Reserve is determined to raise inflation and thereby interest rates and interest rate volatility if it can do so. The long-term debt situation is dire. If history is any guide, new and unexpected challenges will arise.

But the fact that many issues are not pressing makes this moment an ideal one to restructure federal debt. The calm before the storm is a good time to fix the sails.

COMMENT

Darrell Duffie

John Cochrane's proposal for simplifying the debt management of the United States Treasury is original and radical. In its essence, the plan calls for the issuance of only two securities: floating-rate perpetual debt and fixed-rate perpetual debt. This is not merely a proposal for two general "classes" of debt securities. The proposal means literally that Treasury would issue, and keep reissuing over and over, the same two securities, forever! The only issuance decision to be made by Treasury's debt management office would be how much more of each of these same two securities to issue or retire, day by day. Cochrane extends the basic two-security issuance menu by adding their inflation-indexed versions, and considers other possible extensions that I will discuss.

I applaud Cochrane's audacity, clear vision, and goal of simplifying debt management, among other objectives that I do not have space to discuss here. However, his plan is not cost-effective. As I will explain, this extreme restriction on the maturity distribution of outstanding Treasuries would impose a significant cost to the many market participants who have narrow preferences for the maturities of the Treasuries that they choose to own or short. The aversion to owning perpetuals rather than specific-maturity issues would also be reflected in a higher cost to taxpayers for funding the U.S. government. These maturity preferences, sometimes called clientele effects, have been described in prior work—for example Greenwood, Hanson, and Stein (2010) and Krishnamurthy and Vissing-Jorgensen (2012). Most of the relevant literature focuses on preferences only between short-maturity and long-maturity debt, which in principle would be met by Cochrane's stark two-security menu, but the same clientele and liquidity effects described in the prior literature apply to distinctions among many different maturities.

I don't expect much support by market participants for Cochrane's proposal. Both the sell-side and the buy-side of Treasury markets would be apoplectic at the prospect of losing access to large supplies of specific-maturity issues in amounts that are sensitive to their demands for hedging and speculation, especially in light of limits on the liquidity of secondary markets for Treasuries and Treasury repos.

Currently, the Treasury Department is somewhat attentive to the demands of the market for Treasury securities of different maturities in different respective total amounts. To this end, Treasury seeks advice from primary dealers and bodies such as the Treasury Borrowing Advisory Committee. As I will explain, Treasury also infers directly from price signals and daily reports of Treasury delivery failures which particular securities are in especially high demand. Treasury responds by issuing more of those and less of others. Is the U.S. Treasury wasting its time (or even, as Cochrane argues, causing social harm) by catering to the maturity-based demands of Treasury investors? No, it is not.

In an ideal frictionless-market world, as first shown by Wallace (1981), the maturity structure of government debt is irrelevant.[12] All that matters to the real economy is the stream of net cash flows to be spent by the government. The economic effect of any issuance strategy for government liabilities could be costlessly converted by the private sector in this ideal world to the effect of any other issuance strategy that leaves the government with the same net stream of cash flows, through frictionless trading of a full menu of financial contracts.

The Cochrane proposal would at least allow a perpetual fixed-rate note to be "stripped" into a portfolio of coupon-only claims and a forward claim to a perpetual. For example, a perpetual note could be converted to a stream of daily coupon payments for the next ten years and a claim to a perpetual note that starts paying in ten years. Ideally, one could synthesize any desired hypothetical fixed-rate Treasury by packaging the coupon strips accordingly. But the key problem here is not the ability to synthesize a desired position, but rather the available total free float of specific types of notes.

12. Other relevant pieces of this literature include Angeletos (2002), Chamley and Polemarchakis (1984), and Stiglitz (1988).

As I have explained (Duffie 1996), market participants value individual Treasury securities both for the cash flows that they promise and also for liquidity services of various types. In particular, certain benchmark on-the-run Treasuries are often in especially high demand for hedging and speculative purposes. Specific-maturity Treasury bills are also valuable for the defeasance of municipal bonds[13] and other maturity-specific cash management and collateral applications.

Episodically, the demand for certain securities such as the last-issued ("on the run") ten-year Treasury note is so high that in order to obtain these notes one must be willing to lend cash at interest rates below *minus* 2 percent to get owners of the notes to give them up on short-term repos. Even so, there are often not enough of these notes in circulation to meet trading demands, given the limited velocity of their intraday circulation.[14] This often results in cascading failures of sellers to deliver the notes they have promised to buyers.[15] Recently, Treasury has gone so far as to issue the same specific ten-year note in three successive auctions, creating a massive "triple issue" in order to meet the very high demand for these notes, which can be perceived from the special repo-market terms and high rates of delivery failure. There are often similar problems with two-year and five-year notes.

Cochrane recognizes this concern, and considers two potential compromises to his basic perpetuals-only design. Under one variation, Treasury would monitor the market for liquidity pressure on stripped coupon securities at selected maturities and would augment the supply of those strips with special new auctions. I predict, however, that if Treasury were to pursue this route even half as far as its benefits seem to extend, we would end up with a rather heterogeneous maturity profile of outstanding Treasury obligations, running against the spirit of Cochrane's proposal. I would also have some concerns over the lack of liquidity of the many different individual strips, due to thin trading. Over time, a strip whose original maturity had once been in the "sweet spot" would become illiquid. This seems like the sort of problem that Cochrane was actually trying to avoid. In a brief appendix, I discuss another potential intermediate-maturity compromise

---

13. See Ang, Green, and Xing (2013).

14. Vayanos and Weill (2008) provide a search-based model of over-the-counter markets in which even two securities with identical cash flows can be distinguished in price and demand by relative liquidity.

15. See, for example, McCormick (2014).

considered by Cochrane, based on perpetual bonds whose coupon rates decay over time.

A positive aspect of Cochrane's proposal in its purest two-security form is that each of the two perpetuals would be extremely liquid. The entire amount of fixed-rate nominal Treasury debt in existence would trade in the form of a single security, so there would be a super abundance of its supply. For example, even if Treasury decided to issue 90 percent floating-rate debt and only 10 percent fixed-rate perpetuals, the market value of the single fixed-rate perpetual note would exceed $1 trillion at current debt levels, well over ten times the amount of any single Treasury note now in existence. However, an abundant supply of perpetual notes does not mean that the preferences of investors for specific finite-maturity notes are being well served.

What would happen if the Cochrane proposal were adopted? Stripping would be used to create various synthetic Treasury positions whose maturity properties serve specific applications for hedging, speculation, cash management, and collateral. Not all individual strips would be in equally high demand—far from it—but the total supply of traded Treasury fixed-coupon cash flows would be perfectly flat across all maturities. As a result, some strips would trade at notable yield distortions, relative to those suggested by efficient-market term premia. That is, there would be significant liquidity premia, probably much larger than those visible in today's highest-demand Treasury bills and notes, whose supplies are at least somewhat responsive to market demand. The private sector would try to close the gap by creating substitute securities, probably with some degree of success. The opportunity cost to market participants of lost access to a greater amount of maturity-specific Treasuries relative to others would nevertheless be significant.

There is no compelling reason for the government to deny the market the relative quantities of specific-maturity Treasuries that investors demand. The government is able to vary the maturity structure of its debt at a low cost, relative to the benefits of maturity variation to investors. By doing so, the government can lower its interest expense accordingly. While much of the resulting interest-expense savings represent a transfer from Treasury investors to taxpayers, these savings reflect real liquidity benefits to the market.

The best part of Cochrane's proposal for Treasury debt management is the suggestion to create a large outstanding supply of floating-rate notes. Treasury has not come close to satiating the market's extremely high demand for safe, liquid, money-like instruments.[16] In the spirit of my earlier discussion, Treasury could better serve the market by serving more of this demand.

Appendix: Perpetual Bonds with Decaying Coupon Rates

Cochrane's other potential compromise to meet the demand for intermediate-maturity securities would have Treasury issue perpetual notes whose coupon rates decline geometrically with maturity. For example, if the yield curve is flat at some rate y, a perpetual note whose coupons decline at a proportional rate of g per year would have a duration of $1/(r+g)$. Duration, or valued-weighted average maturity, is a standard measure of the sensitivity of the market value of a bond to changes in yields. For example, a perpetual whose coupons decay at 4 percent per year would have a duration of ten years when its yield is 6 percent. A downside, however, is that if recessionary monetary conditions were to push the yield of this note down to 1 percent, its duration would then zoom out to $1/(0.01+0.04)=20$ years. The duration of a conventional ten-year Treasury note would increase only modestly in this scenario, from about 7.7 years when issued at a 6 percent yield to about 8.1 years when its yield drops to 1 percent. From a risk management viewpoint, bond investors generally tend to prefer low duration sensitivity. Treasury would find itself under pressure to issue various bonds with different geometric coupon decay rates to serve various different maturity-specific clienteles, and then to add a further variety of bonds over time in order to compensate for changes in the yield curve. While Treasury could probably maintain adequate liquidity for a relatively rich menu of bonds with different coupon decay rates, this approach seems to defeat much of the simplicity of Cochrane's original scheme. This approach would also raise quite a fuss in the investment community because of the operational costs of dealing with bonds whose coupon income is declining over time.

References

Aguiar, Mark, and Manuel Amador. 2014. "Sovereign Debt," in *Handbook of International Economics*, vol. 4, edited by Elhanan Helpman, Kenneth Rogoff, and Gita Gopinath (Oxford: Elsevier), pp. 647–687.

Ang, Andrew, Richard Green, and Yuang Xing. 2013. "Advance Refundings of Municipal Bonds," working paper (New York: Columbia Business School).

16. See, for example, McCormick (2015).

Angeletos, George. 2002. "Fiscal Policy with Noncontingent Debt and the Optimal Maturity Structure." *Quarterly Journal of Economics* 117: 1105–31.

Atkeson, Andrew, V. V. Chari, and Patrick Kehoe. 1999. "Taxing Capital Income: A Bad Idea." Federal Reserve Bank of Minneapolis, *Quarterly Review* 23: 3–17 (www.minneapolisfed.org/research/qr/qr2331.pdf).

Barro, Robert J. 1999. "Notes on Optimal Debt Management." *Journal of Applied Economics* 2: 281–89.

Borensztein, Eduardo, and Paolo Mauro. 2004. "The Case for GDP-Indexed Bonds." *Economic Policy* 19: 166–216.

Bulow, Jeremy, and Kenneth Rogoff. 1989. "Sovereign Debt: Is to Forgive to Forget?" *American Economic Review* 79: 43–50.

Campbell, John Y., Robert J. Shiller, and Luis M. Viceira. 2009. "Understanding Inflation-Indexed Bond Markets." *Brookings Papers on Economic Activity* (Spring): 79–120 (www.brookings.edu/~/media/projects/bpea/spring%202009 /2009a_bpea_campbell.pdf).

Campbell, John Y., and Luis M. Viceira. 2001. "Who Should Buy Long-Term Bonds?" *American Economic Review* 91: 99–127.

Chamley, Christophe. 1986. "Optimal Taxation of Capital Income in General Equilibrium with Infinite Lives." *Econometrica* 54, no. 3: 607–22.

Chamley, Christophe, and Heracles Polemarchakis. 1984. "Assets, General Equilibrium, and the Neutrality of Money." *Review of Economic Studies* 51: 129–38.

Cochrane, John H. 2001. "Long-Term Debt and Optimal Policy in the Fiscal Theory of the Price Level." *Econometrica* 69, no. 1: 69–116.

———. 2005. "Money as Stock." *Journal of Monetary Economics* 52: 501–28.

———. 2014a. "A Mean-Variance Benchmark for Intertemporal Portfolio Theory." *Journal of Finance* 69: 1–49. doi: 10.1111/jofi.12099.

———. 2014b. "Monetary Policy with Interest on Reserves." *Journal of Economic Dynamics and Control* 49: 74–108.

———. 2014c. "Toward a Run-Free Financial System," in *Across the Great Divide: New Perspectives on the Financial Crisis*, edited by Martin Neil Baily and John B. Taylor (Stanford, Calif.: Hoover Institution Press), pp. 197–249.

Coleman, Thomas S., Lawrence Fisher, and Roger C. Ibbotson. 1993. *Historical U.S. Treasury Yield Curves*. Chicago: Ibbotson Associates.

Debortoli, Davide, Ricardo Nunes, and Pierre Yared. 2014. "Optimal Government Debt Maturity," manuscript, Columbia University (www0.gsb.columbia.edu /faculty/pyared/papers/maturity.pdf), and Working Paper 20632 (Cambridge, Mass.: National Bureau of Economic Research) (www.nber.org/papers /w20632).

Duffie, Darrell. 1996. "Special Repo Rates." *Journal of Finance* 51: 493–526.

Dybvig, Phillip H., and Stephen A. Ross, 1986. "Tax Clienteles and Asset Pricing." *Journal of Finance* 41: 751–62. doi: 10.1111/j.1540-6261.1986.tb04540.x.

Eaton, Jonathan, and Raquel Fernandez. 1995. "Sovereign Debt," in *Handbook of International Economics*, vol. 3, edited by Gene M. Grossman and Kenneth Rogoff (Amsterdam: North-Holland).

Faraglia, Elisa, Albert Marcet, Rigas Oikonomou, and Andrew Scott. 2014. "Government Debt Management: The Long and the Short of It," manuscript, Barcelona GSE Working Paper Series 799 (www.iae.csic.es/investigatorsMaterial/a14512130308archivoPdf31122.pdf).

Friedman, Milton. 1969. "The Optimum Quantity of Money," in *The Optimum Quantity of Money and Other Essays* (Chicago: Aldine), pp. 1–50.

Geddie, John. 2014. "Investors Say GDP Bonds Won't Work." Reuters (www.reuters.com/article/2014/02/21/bonds-gdp-linked-idUSL6N0LN1OG20140221).

Gorton, Gary B., and Guillermo Ordoñez. 2013. "The Supply and Demand for Safe Assets," Working Paper 18732 (Cambridge, Mass.: National Bureau of Economic Research).

Greenwood, Robin Marc, Samuel Gregory Hanson, and Jeremy C. Stein. 2010. "A Comparative-Advantage Approach to Government Debt Maturity," working paper (Cambridge, Mass.: Harvard University).

Harley, C. K. 1976. "Goschen's Conversion of the National Debt and the Yield on Consols." *Economic History Review* 29: 101–6.

Homer, Sidney, and Richard Sylla. 1996. *A History of Interest Rates*, 3rd ed. Rutgers University Press.

Judd, Kenneth L. 1985. "Redistributive Taxation in a Simple Perfect Foresight Model." *Journal of Public Economics* 28: 59–83.

Kamstra, Mark J., and Robert J. Shiller. 2010. "Trills Instead of T-Bills: It's Time to Replace Part of Government Debt with Shares in GDP." *The Economists' Voice* 7, no. 3 (markkamstra.com/papers/Economists-Voice-TrillsInsteadofTBills.pdf).

Kohn, Meir. 1999. "The Capital Market before 1600," manuscript, Dartmouth University (www.dartmouth.edu/~mkohn/Papers/99-06.pdf).

Krishnamurthy, Arvind, and Annette Vissing-Jorgensen. 2012. "The Aggregate Demand for Treasury Debt." *Journal of Political Economy* 120: 233–67.

Lucas, Robert E., Jr. 2003. "Inflation and Welfare." *Econometrica* 68, no. 2: 247–74.

Lucas, Robert E., Jr., and Nancy L. Stokey. 1983. "Optimal Fiscal and Monetary Policy in an Economy without Capital." *Journal of Monetary Economics* 12: 55–93.

Mankiw, N. Gregory, Matthew Weinzierl, and Danny Yagan. 2009. "Optimal Taxation in Theory and Practice." *Journal of Economic Perspectives* 23: 147–74.

McCormick, Liz. 2014. "Treasury Ten-Year Note Repo Shortage Risks Rise in Failed Trades." Bloomberg, June 10 (www.bloomberg.com/news/articles/2014-06-10/treasury-10-year-shortage-risks-trading-fails-rise-nomura-says).

———. 2015. "The $900 Billion Influx That's Wreaking Havoc in U.S. Bills." Bloomberg, May 11 (www.bloomberg.com/news/articles/2015-05-11/the-900-billion-influx-that-s-wreaking-havoc-in-treasury-bills).

Miller, Merton, 1977. "Debt and Taxes." *Journal of Finance* 32: 261–75. doi: 10.1111/j.1540-6261.1977.tb03267.x.

Miyajima, Ken. 2006. "How to Evaluate GDP-Linked Warrants: Price and Repayment Capacity," IMF Working Paper 06/85, March 1 (Washington, D.C.:

International Monetary Fund) (www.imf.org/external/pubs/ft/wp/2006 /wp0685.pdf).

Pancost, N. Aaron. 2015. "Zero-Coupon Yields and the Cross-Section of Bond Prices," March 8 (http://ssrn.com/abstract=2157271 or http://dx.doi.org/10 .2139/ssrn.2157271).

Potter, Simon. 2015. "Challenges Posed by the Evolution of the Treasury Market," remarks at the 2015 Primary Dealer Meeting, New York City, April 13, Federal Reserve Bank of New York (http://newyorkfed.org/newsevents/speeches /2015/pot150413.html).

Schmitt-Grohé, Stephanie, and Martín Uribe. 2004. "Optimal Fiscal and Monetary Policy under Sticky Prices." *Journal of Economic Theory* 114: 198–230.

———. 2005. "Optimal Fiscal and Monetary Policy in a Medium-Scale Macroeconomic Model," in *NBER Macroeconomics Annual 2005*, edited by Mark Gertler and Kenneth Rogoff (Cambridge, Mass.: MIT Press), pp. 383–425.

Sims, Christopher. 2001. "Fiscal Consequences for Mexico of Adopting the Dollar." *Journal of Money, Credit, and Banking* 33: 597–616.

Stiglitz, Joseph B. 1988. "On the Relevance or Irrelevance of Public Financial Policy," in *The Economics of Public Debt* (London: Macmillan), pp. 4–76.

Stubbington, Tommy, and Ben Edwards. 2014. "U.K. to Repay First World War Bonds." *Wall Street Journal*, October 31 (www.wsj.com/articles/u-k-to-repay -first-world-war-bonds-1414745764).

Vayanos, Dimitri, and Pierre-Olivier Weill. 2008. "A Search-Based Theory of the On-the-Run Phenomenon." *Journal of Finance* 63: 1361–98.

Wachter, Jessica. 2003. "Risk Aversion and Allocation to Long-Term Bonds." *Journal of Economic Theory* 112: 325–33.

Wallace, Neal. 1981. "A Modigliani-Miller Theorem for Open-Market Operations." *American Economic Review* 71: 267–74.

Woodford, Michael. 2004. *Interest and Prices*. Princeton University Press.

4

CONCLUDING OBSERVATIONS

Lawrence H. Summers

Policymakers in political environments are most constructive when they find approaches that are appealing from a variety of perspectives and command widespread support. Academics, on the other hand, are most useful when they provoke thought, and you only provoke thought by saying things with which people disagree. For an academic, the number of people who find what you say surprising, unsettling, or irritating is a correlate of success. I am today an economics professor, not a government official, and so my hope is that my concluding comments here will be surprising and unsettling to many.

My work with Greenwood, Hanson, and Rudolph in chapter 1 of this book presents both my views about how debt management policy should be thought about, and about current controversies in debt management policy. Here I offer a number of observations coming out of that research, the various reactions to it, and other reflections on debt management policy, notably those of John Cochrane in this book.

Whether or not one agrees with these observations, it seems to me imperative that debt management policy receive much more attention from the policy community than it has in recent years. Central bank balance sheets are much larger than has been the case traditionally. The payment of interest on reserves

Adapted from comments made at the U.S. Treasury 2014 Roundtable on Treasury Markets and Debt Management, December 5, 2014.

means that reserves are essentially the equivalent of Treasury bills, blurring traditional distinctions between monetary policy and debt management policy. And whether or not one accepts the ideas about secular stagnation that I and others have advanced, the zero lower bound seems likely to be a much more active constraint on monetary policy over the next generation than it has been over the last generation, compelling more consideration of quantitative easing policies that very much overlap with debt management needs policies.

Debt Management in Context

If war is too important to leave to generals, debt management is too important to leave to debt managers, and especially too important to leave to their private sector counterparts.

Debt management decisions are far reaching in their effects. As the enormous controversy over quantitative easing reminds us, debt management decisions have implications not just for government borrowing costs but also for the level of economic activity, the credibility of government efforts to achieve low inflation, the maintenance of financial stability, and the development of capital markets. Given all these ramifications of debt management decisions, they should not be delegated to technocrats who conceive the problem only in terms of maximizing the ease of government borrowing.

A narrow focus on the part of debt managers can and has led them to regard their central constituency as financial institutions that deal in Treasury debt. This in turn reinforces their narrowness of focus as the interests of dealers are, in important respects, divergent from the national interest. Indeed, I sometimes wonder whether the interests of the dealers and Treasury are as much misaligned as they are well aligned. While both have a stake in well-functioning markets, larger bid-ask spreads are profitable for the dealers and expensive for the Treasury. Securities that come in an inconvenient form and need to be financially transformed by the financial community are good for the financial community and an expense from the perspective of the Treasury. Securities that provide a basis for financial innovation are attractive for financial firms but may be threatening to financial stability. Of course, Treasury needs inputs from market participants, but Treasury debt managers will go seriously wrong if they confuse the interests of the Treasury debt community with the national interest.

As important as any of the particular arguments made in this book is the permeating recognition that debt management policy needs to be set in the context of broad macroeconomic policy—certainly in an economy where the zero lower bound is an issue and probably much more generally.

How to Think about Treasury Borrowing Costs

For reasons explained more fully in chapters 1 and 2, I believe that considerable confusion attends most discussions of the maturity structure of Treasury debt, even taking as given their narrow perspective.

It is often baldly stated that the objective of the Treasury is, or ought to be, minimizing expected cost over time. I would have thought that the objective of the Treasury was to minimize risk-adjusted costs. There are any number of actions that participants in well-functioning capital markets can take that have a positive expected return that are nonetheless not thought right to take. For example, an individual, or a firm, or the Treasury can make an expected value profit by selling put options, but this simply is taking on risk and being appropriately compensated. If the Treasury takes on risk on behalf of taxpayers and is compensated less than fairly, it is making a mistake, even if its expected borrowing cost is reduced. It should instead minimize risk-adjusted costs.

This point may be of some significance. In many periods, bond and stock returns are correlated one way or the other. If the Treasury issues longer-term bonds and bears or receives some risk premium that reflects the "beta" of the bonds, this may be wise.

Another point is this: I am convinced that rollover risk treated as an independent issue is mostly a confusion. I recognize that circumstances could arise in which the Treasury would not be able to sell debt, or would be able to sell it only at prohibitive rates. For all relevant purposes, one can think of such times as moments when the interest rate becomes very high or infinite. A proper analysis of cost minimization will recognize that it is very costly to issue debt when rates are very high. And any cost minimization strategy will, if possible, take to zero the probability of having to raise debt when doing so is impossible.

In that regard the frequently expressed conviction that floating-rate debt provides insulation against rollover risk also seems to me a confusion. Imagine that the Treasury suddenly converted half of its short-term debt to floating-rate debt. People who buy the short-term debt at every auction would buy the floating-rate debt instead. At the difficult moment when you had to issue half as much debt as you did before because you have floating-rate debt, you would also have only half as many participants showing up at the auction because they already had the floating-rate debt. So the prospect that you would avoid an interest rate spike is, I believe, a nearly complete confusion. There may be transaction cost reasons—indeed, there probably are—for issuing floating-rate debt, but the idea that floating-rate debt mitigates rollover risk is an error.

The academic literature has devoted enormous attention to considerations around tax smoothing in formulating debt management policies and indeed in thinking more generally about fiscal policy. I find this odd given that the welfare consequences of variations in tax rates are very small. James Tobin famously made the observation that it takes a heap of Harberger triangles to fill an Okun gap as a way of making the point that microeconomic distortions from taxation are small compared to macroeconomic losses from recessions. The welfare losses from variation in tax rates are trivial even compared to the welfare loss from the average level of taxation.

Here is a calculation that illustrates the point. Assume that taxes in the United States represent about 30 percent of GDP, including those at the state and local level. Assume that the deadweight loss from taxation is 15 percent of GDP, which is a fairly high-end estimate, and further assume that the deadweight loss from taxation rises as the square of the tax rate, as is standard. It follows that each incremental dollar of revenue raised generates an equal amount of deadweight loss, so this is taking a very serious view of tax distortions. Then it turns out that the extra loss from varying tax rates between, say, 27 and 33 percent is just 0.3 percent of GDP. Variation of this magnitude is far more than what we observe outside of major wars, and even further beyond what could conceivably come from variations in debt management policies. I conclude that debt managers can, and those who purport to advise them should, outside of wartime ignore tax-smoothing issues in thinking about cost minimization.

And there is one last logical point to make regarding tax smoothing. The presumption that tax smoothing is better accomplished with the issuance of long-term debt is unwarranted. What matters is the real interest rate, not the nominal interest rate. It is not obvious that the real ex-post interest rate on Treasury debt will be more stable or predictable with long-term nominal debt and variable inflation than with floating short-term debt.

The simulations in chapter 1 of this book suggest that the extra uncertainty introduced by moving toward short-term debt is likely to be very, very small. It is my observation that there is a very substantial quantity of private sector activity that is directed to the bond carry trade, that is directed to surfing the yield curve and collecting the resulting term premium, and that is carried out on a substantial scale by thoughtful market professionals who believe that they are being compensated in a way that goes beyond any correlation with the stock market or anything else.

For as long as that is the case, I would establish a strong presumption that Treasury debt management should be shorter than it is. It is certainly possible that if the Treasury issued all short-term debt, the risk would turn negative and at that point, it would be appropriate for the Treasury to be shifting toward more long-term debt. But the basic criteria is, if a trade is really good for hedge funds to make, then it is a bad trade for the Treasury to make on behalf of taxpayers. I believe there is a substantial amount of sophisticated financial activity that in one way or another takes the form of issuing short and lending long. If that is, in fact, the case, it is appropriate for the Treasury, on behalf of taxpayers, to move in the same direction. How far the Treasury could move and have that remain the case is an empirical question. I believe and suspect that the answer is a fair distance.

Reflections on Quantitative Easing

Quantitative easing, which is a kind of debt management policy, has complex effects on economic performance. I am very much aware that there were moments when Ben Bernanke expressed an opinion about QE or a judgment about the future of QE and the next ten minutes were among the most exciting ten minutes in the lives of market participants. So I do not suppose that Robert Barro's neutrality theorem and the like are entirely empirically accurate descriptions of what takes place.[1]

Nonetheless, I would highlight an aspect of the discussion of QE that I find surprising. The price-pressure channel—the notion that Fed purchases of bonds push up their price and, thus, push down their yield—either is important or it is not. I understand how somebody could believe that QE, because it represented a major public effort to purchase long-term bonds, had a substantial effect on reducing long-term bond yields. I understand how the same person could believe that a substantial increase in deficits in the present or in the future could be expected to raise long-term yields substantially because the market would have to absorb much more long-term debt. I do

1. See chapter 1 for a discussion of this theorem.

not, on the other hand, understand the widespread view on the part of my friends that large deficits and their potential impact on long-term yields are a matter of no concern but that QE, through its price-pressure channel, is a vitally important step toward stimulus.

Moreover, as my coauthors and I emphasize in chapter 1, relative to what anybody would have expected, the private markets had to absorb far more long-term Treasury debt than anyone would have found plausible in 2007. Despite the expansion of the Fed's balance sheet, the net effect of what the public sector has done has been to force much more market holding of long-term government debt. Therefore analyses of what's happening in bond markets and stock markets that are premised on the argument that the Fed has expanded its balance sheet by buying a lot of long-term debt miss the highly pertinent empirical observation that the Treasury has done more bond-selling than the Fed has done bond-buying, and the Treasury has almost certainly done more unexpected selling than the Fed has done unexpected buying over the last few years.

Governing Debt Management Policy

I am more confident in the basic notion that there should be some approach the coordination of Treasury and Federal Reserve policy in terms of debt maturity than I was when my colleagues and I were first critical of current arrangements.

John Cochrane and others have impressed on me that the notion of the separation of fiscal and monetary policy is itself a bit of an intellectual confusion. Everybody seems to agree that monetary policy affects various interest rates. Everybody agrees that interest rates affect the government budget constraint, therefore there is no such thing as a monetary policy decision that does not have fiscal policy consequences or, alternatively, if you regard the fiscal policy as initially determinative, there is no such thing as a fiscal policy that does not have monetary policy consequences. The corollary is that there is never going to be a complete independence of monetary and fiscal policy.

The argument for coordination is not, as some caricature it, an assertion that the Treasury should interfere with the Fed's independence. Rather, it is that the Fed should have some influence on what the Treasury does in the debt management area, especially when interest rates are constrained by the zero lower bound.

When at the zero lower interest bound, the Federal Reserve commits itself to pursuing a QE-type policy, what is the consequence of the Treasury deciding at that point to move to term out the debt? It depends on how the Fed responds. One possibility is that the Fed responds passively and doesn't change its QE policy. If that's how the Fed responds, then the consequence is contractionary for aggregate economic activity. It is hard to understand why at moments when the Fed is using QE as an expansionary instrument the Treasury would wish to offset its effects. Certainly no such rationale was ever expressed during the recent episode.

The alternative possibility is that the Fed is in some sense the last mover and follows the Treasury, and the Fed sets the scale of its QE policy to achieve the desired degree of stimulus and thereby offsets any contractionary Treasury policy. If this is what happens, the Treasury's decisions have no impact on either the path of stimulus or the federal budget (given that all Fed profits are rebated to the Treasury). Nonetheless, offsetting Treasury and Fed actions seems inferior to the Fed acting without Treasury offset. With coordination, transaction costs are reduced because there is no need for the private sector to intermediate between the Treasury and the Fed. And the size of the Fed balance sheet and the attendant anxiety it creates is reduced.

Some suggest that any coordination of debt management policy threatens the independence of the Fed. This might be a worry if the Treasury was pressing the Fed for more expansion, as it would raise the concern of the politicization of monetary policy for short-run benefit that leads to support for the independence of central banks. But, in the context here, the issue has been the Treasury offsetting the potential stimulative impact of Fed policies. I can see no legitimate reason why the Fed should not have a voice in encouraging the Treasury to stop doing this.

What Should Be Done?

Finally, if I were not currently an academic trying to provoke and I were Secretary of the Treasury, what would I do about debt management? It would of course depend on the political context, the views of others, and the economic situation. But, I would try to take a number of steps.

First, I would seek to ensure that debt management decisions were made on the basis of overall considerations of economic welfare, not only the functioning of debt markets. Toward this end, I would restructure the Treasury

Borrowing Advisory Committee to give voice to nonfinancial institution stakeholders in debt management decisions. These would include macro-economists who could advise on the impact of debt management decisions on economic activity and regulators who could address the impact of debt management policy on financial stability.

Second, I would instruct debt management officials to review current approaches to determining the maturity distribution of the debt, with a view to reducing profit opportunities for private market participants at the expense of the Treasury. In general I would seek to guide policy toward issuing more debt at maturities where term premiums were low and less at maturities where term premiums were high. At most moments, but possibly not the present, this would likely means shortening the maturity of the debt.

Third, I would seek to reach a new Treasury–Federal Reserve accord on debt management policy appropriate to current conditions. In particular, the fact that the Fed is likely to have a large balance sheet for the foreseeable future and intends to pay interest on reserves, turning them into the equivalent of Treasury bills, represents a profound change in the monetary policy environment. Given that the Treasury and Federal Reserve are part of the same government, it makes no sense for them to independently and separately make decisions about the maturity structure of the outstanding debt. I would propose that except when interest rates were close to zero, the Fed would not engage in policies directed at changing the maturity structure of the debt held by the public. Decisions about debt maturity structure would then fall to the Treasury. On the other hand, when rates were close to zero and so variations in short-term rates were not available as a stabilization tool, I would commit that the Treasury would not act in ways that offset Fed policies unless encouraged to do so by the Fed.

Of course, a great deal of effort would have to go into formulating these principles precisely, and there would be operational details to work out. But I would push very hard for some set of principles that ensured that one country had one debt management policy.

CONTRIBUTORS

STEPHEN G. CECCHETTI
Professor of International Economics, Brandeis International Business School; member of Advisory Council, Hutchins Center for Fiscal and Monetary Policy, Brookings Institution

JOHN H. COCHRANE
Senior Fellow, Hoover Institution, Stanford University

JASON CUMMINS
Chief U.S. Economist and Head of Research, Brevan Howard Inc.

DARRELL DUFFIE
Dean Witter Distinguished Professor of Finance at the Graduate School of Business, and Professor (by courtesy), Department of Economics, Stanford University

JANICE EBERLY
James R. and Helen D. Russell Distinguished Professor of Finance, Kellogg School of Management, Northwestern University

ROBIN GREENWOOD
George Gund Professor of Finance and Banking, Harvard Business School

SAMUEL G. HANSON
Assistant Professor, Finance Unit, Harvard Business School

PAUL MCCULLEY
Chairman, Global Society of Fellows, Global Interdependence Center; former Managing Director and Chief Economist, PIMCO

MARY JOHN MILLER
Former Under Secretary of the Treasury for Domestic Finance, U.S. Department of the Treasury; former Director of the Fixed Income Division, T. Rowe Price

JOSHUA S. RUDOLPH
Master in Public Policy, Harvard Kennedy School of Government

BRIAN SACK
Director of Global Economics, The D. E. Shaw Group; former Executive Vice President, Federal Reserve Bank of New York

LAWRENCE H. SUMMERS
Charles W. Eliot University Professor, Harvard University

DAVID WESSEL
Director, Hutchins Center on Fiscal and Monetary Policy, Brookings Institution

INDEX

Made in the USA
Monee, IL
15 March 2025

14023657R00104